OUR
MANY
SELVES

OUR
MANY
SELVES

Elizabeth O'Connor

1817

Harper & Row, Publishers, San Francisco

New York, Grand Rapids, Philadelphia, St. Louis
London, Singapore, Sydney, Tokyo, Toronto

For Dick, twin and companion
of my growing up, whose divided
self keeps me close to suffering,

and

for all those who labor that
the mentally ill may know wholeness.

LIBRARY OF CONGRESS CATALOG CARD NUMBER: 78-124699

90 91 92 93 94 95 MPC 30 29 28 27 26 25 24 23 22 21

CONTENTS

PART THREE

ACKNOWLEDGMENTS

Acknowledgment is made to the following for permission to reprint materials as indicated:

ANN ELMO AGENCY, INC. for extract from *The Self in Pilgrimage* by Earl A. Loomis, Jr.

ASSOCIATION PRESS for extracts from *The Holy Spirit in Five Worlds* and *Religious Dimensions of Personality* by Wayne E. Oates.

ATHENEUM PUBLISHERS, INC. for extract from *The Image:* A Guide to Pseudo-Events in America, by Daniel J. Boorstin. Copyright © 1961 by Daniel J. Boorstin. Reprinted by permission of Atheneum Publishers. Available in the Harper Colophon paperback edition.

BASIC BOOKS, INC. for extract from *The Collected Papers of Sigmund Freud,* edited by Ernest Jones, M.D., Basic Books, Inc., Publishers, New York, 1959. Permission also of Sigmund Freud Copyrights Ltd., The Institute of Psycho-Analysis and The Hogarth Press Ltd. (Vol. XIV of the *Standard Edition of the Complete Psychological Works of Sigmund Freud*).

GEOFFREY BLES LTD. for extracts from *The Destiny of Man* by Nicolas Berdyaev.

CAMBRIDGE UNIVERSITY PRESS for extracts from *The New English Bible with the Apocrypha,* © The Delegates of the Oxford University Press and The Syndics of the Cambridge University Press, 1961, 1970. Reprinted by permission.

DELACORTE PRESS for extract from *The Master Game* by Robert S. de Ropp. Copyright © 1968 by Robert S. de Ropp. A Seymour Lawrence Book/Delacorte Press. Used by permission.

THE DIAL PRESS for extract from *Search for the New Land* by Julius Lester. Copyright © 1969 by Julius Lester and used by permission of the publisher.

DOUBLEDAY & COMPANY, INC. for extract from *No Bars to Manhood* by

Daniel Berrigan. Copyright © 1960 by Daniel Berrigan. Reprinted by permission of Doubleday & Company, Inc.

DOVER PUBLICATIONS, INC. for extract from *Tragic Sense of Life* by Miguel De Unamuno, 1921. Reprinted by permission of the publisher.

FARRAR, STRAUS & GIROUX, INC. for extract from *The Search Within* by Theodor Reik, © 1956.

GROVE PRESS, INC. for extract from *Games People Play:* The Psychology of Human Relationships, by Eric Berne, © 1964.

HARCOURT BRACE JOVANOVICH, INC. for extracts from *In Search of the Miraculous* by P. D. Ouspensky, © 1949.

HARPER & ROW for extracts from *The Inner World of Choice* by Frances G. Wickes. Copyright © 1963 by Frances G. Wickes; for extracts from *Treatises and Sermons of Meister Eckhart* by James M. Clark and John V. Skinner. Copyright © by James Midgley Clark and John Vass Skinner 1958; for extracts from *The Life and Death of Dietrich Bonhoeffer* by Mary Bosanquet. Copyright © 1968 by Mary Bosanquet; for extract from *Life Together* by Dietrich Bonhoeffer, translated by John Doberstein. Copyright 1954 by Harper & Row; for extracts from *Shantung Compound* by Langdon Gilkey. Copyright © 1966 by Langdon B. Gilkey; for extract from *To a Dancing God* by Sam Keen. Copyright © 1970 by Sam Keen; for extract from *Apology for Wonder* by Sam Keen. Copyright © 1969 by Sam Keen; for extracts from *A Testament of Devotion* by Thomas R. Kelly. Copyright 1941 by Harper & Row; for extract from *Purity of Heart Is to Will One Thing,* Rev. Ed., by Søren Kierkegaard, translated by Douglas V. Steere. Copyright 1938, 1948 by Harper & Row; for extract from *The New Man for Our Time* by Elton Trueblood. Copyright © 1970 by Elton Trueblood; for extracts from *The Spirit and the Forms of Love* by Daniel Day Williams. Copyright © 1968 by Daniel Day Williams.

HARVARD EDUCATIONAL REVIEW for extract from "Person to Person: The Problem of Being Human" by Carl Rogers.

HERDER & HERDER for extract from *The Prison Meditations of Father Alfred Delp,* Published by Herder & Herder, 232 Madison Avenue, New York 10016; for extracts from *Suffering* by Louis Evely, Published by Herder & Herder, 232 Madison Avenue, New York 10016.

HOLT, RINEHART AND WINSTON, INC. for extract from *The Search for Authenticity* by J. F. T. Bugental.

THE INSTITUTE OF JESUIT SOURCES for extract from *A Modern Scriptural Approach to the Spiritual Exercises* by David M. Stanley.

ALFRED A. KNOPF, INC. for extract from *The Doctor and the Soul* by

ACKNOWLEDGMENTS

Viktor E. Frankl, trans. by Richard and Clara Winston. Copyright © 1955, 1965 by Alfred A. Knopf, Inc. Reprinted by permission of the publishers; for extract from *Markings* by Dag Hammarskjöld. Copyright © 1964 by Alfred A. Knopf, Inc. and Faber & Faber Ltd. Reprinted by permission of Alfred A. Knopf, Inc.; for extract from *The Human Mind* by Karl Menninger. Copyright 1930, 1937, 1945 and renewed 1958, 1965 by Karl Menninger. Reprinted by permission of Alfred A. Knopf, Inc.

J. B. LIPPINCOTT COMPANY for extract from *The True Wilderness* by H. A. Williams. Copyright © 1965 by H. A. Williams. Reprinted by permission of J. B. Lippincott Company.

THE MACMILLAN COMPANY for extract from *The Informed Heart* by Bruno Bettelheim, © 1960 by The Free Press, a Corporation; for extracts from *Letters and Papers from Prison,* Rev. Ed., by Dietrich Bonhoeffer. Copyright 1953 by The Macmillan Company; © SCM Press, Ltd. 1967; extract from *The New Testament in Modern English,* © by J. B. Phillips, 1958.

THE MINNESOTA REVIEW for poem "Eunice" by Sheila Alexander.

NATIONAL COUNCIL OF THE CHURCHES OF CHRIST IN THE U.S.A. for extracts from the Revised Standard Version Bible.

THE NEW YORK TIMES for "Light in Darkness" by Dr. Howard A. Rusk, Jan. 4, 1959.

W. W. NORTON & COMPANY, INC. for extracts from *New Ways in Psychoanalysis* by Karen Horney, M.D.

OXFORD UNIVERSITY PRESS for extracts from *The Oxford Dictionary of Quotations.*

PANTHEON BOOKS for extracts from *The Psychology of Power* by R. V. Sampson. Copyright © 1965 by R. V. Sampson. Reprinted by permission of Pantheon Books, Inc. a Division of Random House, Inc.

PENGUIN BOOKS LTD. for extract from *The Integrity of Personality* by Anthony Storr.

PRINCETON UNIVERSITY PRESS for extracts from *The Collected Works of C. G. Jung,* ed. by G. Adler, M. Fordham, H. Read, tr. by R. F. C. Hull; for extracts from *The 'I' and the 'Not-I'* by M. Esther Harding.

G. P. PUTNAM'S SONS for extracts from *Jung's Contribution to Our Time* by Eleanor Bertine; for extracts from *Depth Psychology and a New Ethic* by Erich Neumann. Copyright © 1969 by Hodder & Stoughton Ltd. and The C. J. Jung Foundation for Analytical Psychology.

RANDOM HOUSE, INC. for extract from *Heroic Heart* by Kim Malthe-Bruun, trans. by Gerry Bothner. Copyright 1955 by Random House, Inc. Reprinted by permission of the publisher.

SATURDAY REVIEW for extract from "The Challenge of Fear" by Alan Paton, September 9, 1967 *Saturday Review*.

SCHOCKEN BOOKS INC. for extract from *Tales of the Hasidim: Early Masters* by Martin Buber. Copyright © 1947 by Schocken Books Inc., for extract from *Tales of the Hasidim: Later Masters* by Martin Buber. Copyright © 1948 by Schocken Books Inc.; for extract from *Ten Rungs* by Martin Buber. Copyright © 1947 by Schocken Books Inc.

SCM PRESS LTD. for extract from *The Altar Fire* by Olive Wyon.

SHEED & WARD INC. for extract from *The Complete Works of Saint Teresa*.

SIMON & SCHUSTER, INC. for extract from *The Chosen* by Chaim Potok, © 1967 by Chaim Potok and reprinted by permission of Simon & Schuster, Inc.

UNITED CHURCH PRESS for extract from *The Power of the Provisional* by Roger Schutz, trans. Philip Parsons and Timothy Wilson. English translation copyright © 1969 by Hodder & Stoughton; American rights, United Church Press.

VAN NOSTRAND REINHOLD COMPANY for extract from *Creativity and Conformity* by Clark Moustakas. Copyright © 1967 by Clark E. Moustakas, by permission of Van Nostrand Reinhold Company.

THE VIKING PRESS INC. for extract from *After the Fall* by Arthur Miller.

VINCENT STUART & JOHN M. WATKINS LTD. for extracts from *Psychological Commentaries* by Maurice Nicoll.

WESLEYAN UNIVERSITY PRESS for "Divided, the Man is Dreaming." Copyright © 1965 by John Haines. Reprinted from *Winter News* by John Haines, by permission of Wesleyan University Press.

THE WESTMINSTER PRESS for extract from *The Face of the Deep* by Charles B. Hanna. Copyright © MCMLXVII, The Westminster Press. Used by permission.

THE WORLD PUBLISHING COMPANY for extracts from *Coming into Existence: The Struggle to Become an Individual* by Raymond Rogers. Copyright © 1967 by Raymond Rogers; extract from *The Acting Approach* by George Weinberg.

Acknowledgment is made to the following persons for permission to reprint material from their writings:
Alexander Dru for extract from his translation of *Journals of Kierkegaard;* John Howard Griffin for extract from *Creative Suffering;* E. Graham Howe for extracts from *The Open Way* by E. Graham Howe and L. Le Mesurier; Elined Kotschnig for "Creative Light"; Elsie Landstrom for "Song to My Other Self"; Rolland R. Reece for extract from *Notes from a Journal;* Wayne E. Oates for extract from *Anxiety in Christian Experience*.

PREFACE

The exercises in this book were originally written to be used in the mission groups that staff the Potter's House, which is the coffee house of The Church of The Saviour. The Potter's House was in a time of transition. For nine years it had operated on Columbia Road, which was once a modest, nondescript thoroughfare in the nation's capital. In the first years of the Potter's House business groups and civic organizations used it frequently as a place of meeting. In those days model plans for the neighborhood were debated and fought, but this is almost forgotten now.

Long before the riots of the spring of 1968 signs of deterioration became visible on the street. They were discernible almost week by week. First one theater closed; then the second stopped showing first-run movies. Small businesses began to disappear. Larger ones made plans to move to the suburbs. One resident commented, "When money begins to leave an area, it's like being in the wake of a storm." Our street began to have a scarred and dismayed look. In

1968 the Potter's House Gift Shop, located two blocks from the coffee house, was held up for the second time; shoplifting consistently depleted its inventory, and finally it closed. Outside the doors dope peddling, crime, and fear grew. Our street mirrored the crisis of our city and the crises of all urban areas.

Did the Potter's House have a ministry any longer, and if so, what was it? Out of the struggle for those answers came a renewed commitment to the city. Encouraged by other groups that were working to make the city livable for its people, the seventy members and intern members of the Potter's House pledged themselves to labor for the rebuilding of Washington. Inspiration had come from the words of James W. Rouse, the developer and builder of the planned city of Columbia, Maryland, between Washington and Baltimore. *Life* magazine had called him the messianic Master Builder. It was easy to see why when he spoke about the city. He was alive with what it could be, and in his presence others began to image a different kind of city and believe that it was possible. "We are caught," he said, "in our own trap because we have never seen a good big city in our time." He defined as major obstacles the attitudes of hopelessness, disbelief, and despair with which we approach the city. Speaking in our coffee house in May 1969, he said,

More deeply ingrained in us than we know is an acceptance of the fact that cities do not work and basically none of us expects them to work, from the President of the United States straight on down to the social worker and all the people engaged in the task of the city. There is no one on the job who believes that we are really going to win the battle of making the city an effective place for a man and his wife to raise a family. The evidence of this is on every hand. . . . Not one city in America has even contemplated victory. Nobody asks, "What would this city be like, if it really worked?" And yet is not this fantastically ridiculous in the most advanced productive civilization in the history of man? . . . Why in so many places do we stand helpless before the task of providing a suitable environment for people to live in? . . . This is rapidly meaning all the people of America. In 1940 roughly 40 per cent of our people lived in cities; in 1980, 80 per cent will live in cities. In the next twenty years 70 million people will be added to the cities.

Mr. Rouse did not give us any plans or strategy. He did transmit, however, his own contagious spirit of hope. It was clearer that our task was to be ourselves conveyors of hope. It seemed more urgent than before that the Potter's House be a people and a place sharing in a vision of an awakened city that would nurture life in its people. While we worked for the viable forms that would enable our young men to see visions and our old to dream again, task forces began to form to deal with problems of hunger and housing. Since its inception the coffee house existed to encourage dialogue. Now that dialogue focused on making new the city.

Deep in us we knew, however, that the transformation of a city was dependent on transformed people and that finally a commitment to the building of the city had to involve a commitment to change in us. We began to reflect on what this meant as we had so many times before when we were expanding our activities beyond our existing structures.

Just about that time Erich Fromm's *The Revolution of Hope* was published,[1] proposing a movement that would have at its core small, decentralized groups that would develop a new style of life and be committed to projects which would offset the life-eroding compulsion of our technological age. He did not attempt to define the new forms of living or group activities, but raised a question as to whether there was a sufficient number of persons who cared enough to become a "radically committed minority."

His book was further confirmation of the call we were feeling to the city. Most of us said in our conversations together that the Potter's House must have at its heart a "radically committed minority." We wanted what it implied for our own lives as well as for the mission to the city. We began to ponder its meaning in terms of the ancient disciplines of Christians.

Once again we renewed our commitment to intercession for one another and the city which we had claimed for our parish. We knew there was no ministry of power without hours spent in the silence waiting for the imparting of God's Spirit and direction. We also

1. New York: Harper & Row, 1968.

knew that prayer was costly and that we would resist it. We had grown wise enough, however, not to rush out and buy a new book on prayer. Time had taught us that no inspiring talk or book was going to make a difference for long. Our need was the practical application of the books we had already read. The real establishment that needed to be overthrown was not the Welfare Department or the complacent affluent or the slum landlords, but the establishment in each of us that had its own dole system, that did not want to be denied its little comforts and had condemned the real self to a dim and dingy cellar. The question was not whether we were committed to prayer, but what help and support we were willing to give each other. What corporate disciplines would be of use? What could we do to dethrone the power within that was intent on another way and had a passion for keeping things as they were? "The violent take the Kingdom." Was there in us a small militant band that could be encouraged and strengthened? How much accountability would be supportive?

We struggled with the same questions as we looked at Scripture. How do we read this Book so that we are changed by it? How do we read it so that the Pharisees in us, who will not let the new come but cling to their old traditions and ways of responding, are shaken out of their strongholds? What does it mean to be a "radically committed minority" at the point of Scripture?

Other questions were asked as we considered our corporate style of life. We were all involved in covenants of family, work, and community. Could we even say, as we once had, that we had unlimited liability for each other? Or did other demands make that unreal? How would we handle conflict and anger within the groups? What did it mean to be honest—to speak the truth in love? And what about money—where were we hung up at this point? How did we really feel about putting our money where our words were? And what about time—were we already pressured by too many requests coming to us as demand? What about sex, in an age of shifting values where the pendulum was completing its swing from renunciation to unrestricted freedom? What about authority? Were

we willing to exercise it? Were we willing to give it to others? The
classical disciplines of poverty, chastity, and obedience were being
raised again as they always will be when the Church becomes serious. Only now they were under the headings of money, sex, and
authority. What was the corporate style of a "radically committed
minority" in the twentieth century? How were we to be a people
growing in consciousness? The people of the Way were a people
who had awakened to hidden depths in themselves. Membership in
the Church would have to mean this again, if the Church was to
reclaim its revolutionary role in society. What were the structures
that would enable the Church to be a laboratory for change?

These and a hundred other questions we explore and wrestle
with to develop a style of life that will help nurture growth in
ourselves and make us more available to each other and to our
city. The exercises in this book are some of those we have used as
one way to be on an inward journey. Others on money, envy, prayer,
and gifts will be published in a companion volume. The exercises
here may seem to emphasize our dark dimensions, but it is in order
that light may break and we may be born into freedom and joy.
Strangely enough we strengthen love in ourselves when we raise
into full consciousness the shadow side of our lives. Conversely,
when we keep negative feelings out of sight, they smother the love
that seems to lie deeper and closer to the real self. This is probably
why there is so much pain in not loving. The life that is not able to
express the love which is integral to it grows deformed.

In Romans 13:8 (RSV), it is written "Owe no one anything,
except to love one another." In writing this volume I have obeyed
that command, for I find myself heavily in the debt of love: to the
members of my mission group who pray for me and the interaction
of whose lives with mine gave me some of the content of this book;
to Kathryn Campbell for her long hours of editing and work on the
bibliography; to Barbara Johnson, Marilyn Funkhouser, Bill Ham,
Dick and Elizabeth White, who were gentle critics; to Jean Sense-
man, Carolyn Wright, Mary Romeyn, Sonya Dyer, and Marjorie
Pevey, who gave helpful support in typing, reading, and proof-

reading; to Gordon Cosby, who is always my good counselor; to Hugh Ripman for his wisdom and the privilege of being for a short time his student; to the authors of the writings in this book, which have for a long time guided my own inward journey; and finally to Dorothy Ham, whose love and encouragement were essential contributions to the preparation of this book. To all I want to acknowledge my debt and express my warmest gratitude.

HOW TO USE
THE EXERCISES

1. The exercises are intended to give us practice in observing and meditating on our own lives. They can be used alone, with one other person, or as group assignments. Some have been used as meditative material on retreats. If you agree to work on the exercises with another person, it would be helpful to establish a regular time when you meet to exchange your experiences. This would also apply to groups which form for the purpose of working with them. If they are introduced into the structure of existing groups, ample time in the group meeting should be designated for sharing the work that each person does during the week.

2. Reserve a half hour each day, preferably at the same time and in the same place, for reflection and self-examination. Meditate on several of the readings which follow each exercise, on your own life, and on God.

3. The selections for meditative reading are not meant to guide you along someone else's path, but to help you find your own. They

suggest questions and material for self-examination. Some are simply to offer encouragement. No attempt is made to exhaust what can be said on a subject. Let the readings be a stepping-off place for your meditation that will give you your own questions and answers and guide. Practice in meditative reading is not only to hear what an author is saying, but to give our own thoughts and feelings an opportunity to be fully heard. This means we expose ourselves to the possibility of change; whenever we listen to ourselves or to another we take this risk.

4. A minimum of one week is suggested for each exercise. If you feel strongly that there is no profit in staying a whole week with a given exercise, move on to the next. If more time is needed, the week may be extended. Be quicker, however, to lengthen the time than to shorten it. Self-examination and meditative reading are forms of prayer which are learned through consistent practice over a long time. Because they are difficult arts to master, it is important that regular times be established for the practice of them. (If you are working in a group, be subject to the direction of your leader. There are other dimensions of prayer that some will want to add that are not considered here because of the limitations of this book.)

5. Whatever the disciplines you decide on, they should be related to the goals that you establish for yourself in connection with the work on the exercises. To be helpful, disciplines must be tied in with your life and where you want to go. This will not make them easy, but it will make it possible for you to struggle with them in difficult circumstances. The steps of the inner life are only for those who are conscious of a level of life different from the one on which they are living. What often happens is that disciplines are pressed on those who may not be on any journey at all and are quite content where they are. In this way what helps some to be born into freedom becomes the means for delivering others into slavery. That slavery may account in part for this age's rebellion against the ordered life. When we find goals again, then we will be able to talk more easily about these things. Whenever we become serious about our aims in life, disciplines begin to take on positive

meanings and cease to throw us into negative states. This does not mean that they will no longer cause rebellion in us. It is the nature of discipline to create friction. The word is derived from the Latin *discere,* which means to learn. Always there will be a self in us that will resist knowing about the new, a self that wants to keep things as they are and cannot bear to look a fact in the face. If you choose disciplines that are concerned with change in you, they will awaken all kinds of resistances that you might have stayed blissfully unaware of. It is in the fire of this struggle that one's many selves become united in a single aim.

When disciplines no longer help us to confront the darkness and division in ourselves, or become disassociated from our goals, they cease to serve us and we begin to serve them. It is essential to remember that they have no value in themselves. If the reason for them is lost and cannot be recovered, throw them out as useless. We should hesitate, however, to discard a discipline on the basis of the resistance or rebellion of one of our many selves, for if it does its work, it will raise protest in us and point out the places of our withholding. Very few ever make these discoveries.

We sometimes have the feeling that disciplines do not serve us well if they give us pain. Nothing could be further from the truth. I hesitate to call attention to the tired example of the athlete whose rigorous program causes him the pain of conditioning and stretching muscles; but the disciplines of the athlete, the financier, the musician, the student, are much easier to understand than those of a man who wants to climb a mountain in himself.

Throw disciplines out when you have lost sight of your mountain. Throw them out when they wound you and make you unfit to climb. But cling to them when they show you what you must overcome to reach what is high in yourself.

6. St. Ignatius, in the Introductory Observations to his exercises, suggests that "It will be very profitable for the one who is to go through the Exercises to enter upon them with magnanimity and generosity toward his Creator and Lord, and to offer Him his entire will and liberty, that His Divine Majesty may dispose of him and

all he possesses according to His most holy will." Though the words have an ancient sound, the suggestion still merits attention. God is the God of our unconscious as well as the God of our conscious. It will be very profitable to commit into His hands each day the self you know and ask Him, if it is His will, to deliver into your keeping that day a part of the self you do not know. This is redemption.

7. Do not put the exercise aside when you have finished your meditation, but carry it around with you during the day. The more attention you give to it, the more it will instruct and help you to become aware of your feelings. It will help not only in learning to observe yourself, but in being present to yourself and to others. What you discover in the midst of your activities can be material for pondering and more careful examination during times of meditation.

8. When you begin a new exercise, it does not mean that you will lose awareness of the old. One that you have already worked with and considered carefully will present itself to your memory at times when it can be of help. Periodically you may want to work with it again in a more disciplined way. The exercises cover subjects that one way or another will concern you all your life. When you return to one, you will find that you have changed and that your understanding of what you read has changed. You will discover different aspects of yourself. Also, you will find that your sharing with another, or in a group, is at a different level. More trust will have been established, and you will be willing to take larger risks.

9. The exercises have not accomplished their purpose if they discourage you or make you feel guilty. There are enough things in life to do that. Do not use the readings to discern what rung of some spiritual ladder you may be on. There is no place where you should be. The exercises are to help you on the journey of becoming more conscious. That journey begins wherever you are. The God you find at the beginning is not different from the God you will find at the end. His word is the same in both places. You are accepted as you are.

10. A most profitable discipline to adopt as you work with these exercises is the keeping of a journal. Keep it for your own sake and your own eyes, so that you write in it without reservations. Let it be a description of your inner world and what is happening there. Put in it all the feelings you are aware of—feeling of love and hate and fear. Include what you unearth by your meditation. Write in it your prayers, your resolutions, the little dialogues you have with yourself, your dreams, your fantasies, your response to events and people. Let it be representative of both your spiritual and your psychological odyssey, if you separate the two. Always include what you have observed about yourself as you worked with an exercise. If your way of communication is art, then make it an art journal. When you look back and read it, you will discover recurring themes and questions that will be helpful to consider further in times of meditation. Your journal is another way of being in dialogue with your many selves.

PART ONE

OUR MANY SELVES

It was during a time of painful conflict that I first began to experience myself as more than one. It was as though I sat in the midst of many selves. Some urged me down one path and some another. Each presented a different claim and no self gave another self an opportunity to be fully heard. In quiet meeting with friends I would often be made aware of the conflicting voices within. When it was my turn to join in the talk or initiate conversation, I would miss the opportunity. I would think, "I will say this," and another self would intrude and have a very different subject for which it demanded attention. And when I assented to speak for it there pushed to the fore still another self with another claim. While I listened to one and then the other, the conversation outside me went on to other things, and none of my selves found a spokesman in me. To others I seemed sometimes far removed, and it was true. I had been called away to attend to an inner clamor—the voices of my own many selves.

The sharper the disunity in one's self, the more one is able to observe the many selves. Events can be so disrupting that we experience our life as shattered, and have obviously the task of finding the pieces and making it whole. In the way through that crisis to a new integration, the perception is heightened so that we see in clear relief the different parts of the self. But today it does not take a crisis situation to see our inner division. Even in ordinary circumstances, the tensions are such that many have the feeling of being fragmented and having to collect themselves. Our times are pointing us toward a deeper definition of the Hebrew word *shalom* as the experience of inner unity—of being one.

When I became aware that I was not one, I began to find in poetry and drama allusions to the multiplicity of selves. "I am large," cried Walt Whitman, "I contain a multitude." There had, of course, always been this kind of reference in literature, but there was nothing alive in me for it to take hold of. I had heard of the prophetic voice in poetry; now I identified that voice for myself. Not only were the poets confirming my own experience of the many selves, but they became for me forerunners of an age to come in which the division within will be more common knowledge than it is today.

And then, in Scripture, I began to hear the same cry, "My name is Legion!"[1] but in Scripture it was more than a solitary utterance here and there. Parables and stories and teachings all concerned the possibility of man attaining to an inner unity. Suddenly it seemed that this was what Christianity was all about—the "Single One" as opposed to the man with a divided heart. "How long will you go limping with two different opinions?"[2] was more than Elijah's question. It was the question of the whole New Testament. The early Church was confronting men with their inner division so that there might be a healing of it.

My own understanding of the concept of the many selves was deepened when I was introduced to a small group outside the

1. Mark 5:9 (RSV).   2. 1 Kings 18:21 (RSV).

church which was working with the teachings of Georges Gurdjieff. I began to meet regularly with the group and to read books on the system of ideas which is known as the Work. I first discovered *In Search of the Miraculous,* P. D. Ouspensky's account of his meeting with Gurdjieff and his eight years as his pupil.[3] After this I began reading the *Psychological Commentaries* of the Jungian analyst Maurice Nicoll.[4] All five volumes of the commentaries are on the teachings of Gurdjieff and Ouspensky. I have not yet finished reading them, because they are books you not only read, but work with.

Gurdjieff believed that no one gained anything without having to struggle and to overcome obstacles. He never made it easy for people to be in touch with him or his work groups. He would sometimes arrive in St. Petersburg from a distant city and call one of his pupils and instruct him to circulate the information that there would be a meeting that evening. There was consternation on the part of those who lived too far outside of St. Petersburg to get there, or who had not time to arrange for children or other household matters. Ouspensky quotes Gurdjieff as having said, "People do not value what is easily come by, and if a man has already felt something, believe me, he will sit waiting all day at the telephone in case he should be invited. Or he will himself ring up and ask and inquire. And whoever expects to be asked, and asked beforehand so that he can arrange his own affairs, let him go on expecting."[5]

With books on Gurdjieff's teachings I find myself adopting his style. I rarely speak of them and I never press them on to others, which is my usual way with books I find helpful. I have had the feeling that they should be put only into the hands of those who ask. This is more than my being an obedient pupil; I am convinced that what has the greatest meaning for us is what we uncover for ourselves. And also that he who seeks, does indeed find. This hints of guardian angels and mysterious signs that point us in the way we are to go. So be it! I confess that one of my many selves believes in

3. New York: Harcourt, Brace & Co., 1949. 4. London: Vincent Stuart, 1964.
5. Ouspensky, op. cit., p. 31.

a universe that is inhabited by spirits. It is unimpressed that modern psychology finds them to be projections of the psyche. What does that mean except that they also have an inner reality? Because of this self I am not at all certain that churches need the billboards out front that announce the services at 9:00 and 11:00, and the sermon, and the text. I am not sure that churches need the listings in the classified directory nor the advertisements in the Saturday newspapers. The mystic self in me knows that wherever the hunger of people is fed, word of it is carried to those who are hungry.

There is also a fearful self in me that made it easy to keep secret for a time my findings of the teachings of Gurdjieff. This self loves the approval of men and does not like to admit that it has looked for truth in unorthodox places. It wants to live up to the expectations of others, and meet their standards and walk in the paths they have established as the proper paths. This self loves permanency— permanent friends, permanent home, permanent job, permanent love. It knows very little about the Gospel and a pilgrim people who have no place to lay their heads and tomorrow may be delivered up to magistrates. Though it struggles hard to dominate the scene, and sometimes succeeds, it is usually won over by my tent-dwelling self, which would be glad to live out of a suitcase. This self will not be contained within neat boundaries. Its Lord is the one who said, "The truth will make you free."[6] It cleaves to this and moves toward having the world as its domain. In the mouth of the pariah, the storefront preacher, the speaker in tongues, the Quaker and the Zen Buddhist, it finds the beckoning presence of its Lord. It has discovered that truth can reside in packages of lostness, and that there are no mimeographed directions to the house of the Teacher.

The tent-dweller in me needs the fearful ones to help it see the temporal order of things. Otherwise it might get the unearthly, wraithlike stare of those who peer into the distance and never see what is at hand. This is probably one of the reasons the instructions are so clear that if any want to build a tower, they should first sit

6. John 8:32 (RSV).

down and work out the cost of it, to see if they can afford to finish it.⁷ It takes the sentimentality out of vision, and for this we need conversation with fearful selves. The pilgrim self also needs the fearful ones to remind it that it cannot survive in its own strength alone, that it needs the company of those who have been in touch with what is highest in themselves. This self does not find archaic the ancient concept of communion with the saints. In that communion it learns that there is no abandonment. "Lo, I am with you always."⁸ There is, after all, one permanent love. In that love it finds its perspective and learns to assign to proper places those selves that would persuade it into narrower, safer ways where all friends are kept, and lands and house are secured, and no Lazarus returns with any warning.⁹

As I worked with the writings of Nicoll I came to a more conscious recognition of the plurality in myself and in every man. The concept of the many I's came alive in me, so that I began to think about the ways in which this idea might affect our relationship with ourselves and each other if it were to become widely accepted. I do not know enough about this system of ideas which Gurdjieff and his present-day disciples teach to want to do anything but acknowledge their influence. Some of those teachings are of an esoteric nature and do not reach anything in me, but others have deepened my understanding of the Church and Christianity, though this may not have been in their design. There was nothing startlingly new in the teachings. It was simply that my study of them raised to a new level of consciousness what I already knew, or was on the verge of knowing. The ideas that had most appeal I had come across before in religious writings and in psychoanalytical literature. Here, however, they seemed to be developed in such a way as to give important tools to the person in search of self-knowledge. One of the ideas stressed over and over was that there is no self-knowledge without self-observation. Certainly there is nothing new in that concept, and yet it is possible to agree with it and have only a surface under-

7. Luke 14:28.   8. Matt. 28:20 (RSV).
9. Luke 16.

standing of how profound an idea it is and how essential it is to real self-knowledge. Even to grasp the significance of it does not assure that one will be able to do it. Self-observation requires practice and structures that remind and hold one accountable.

One of the dividends of psychoanalysis or of group therapy is that one develops the ability to be an observer of his own feelings and his responses to situations as they happen in him, rather than forty-eight hours later, if at all. In so many books on psychoanalysis the hope is expressed that a person will continue his movement toward wholeness after therapy stops. This can be said with some confidence when he has developed an ability to be an observer of himself and to be in more immediate touch with his feelings. Self-observation is the groundwork for self-knowledge, and it is self-knowledge that effects change. This is a very ordinary kind of fact, but it has not yet been used extensively to give the help so desperately sought today. Certainly it is understanding that can be used in the small-group movement within the church; we can be given week-in and week-out practice in the art of self-observation. There is no reason why help in that art need be limited to a strictly therapeutic situation—it might even begin in elementary school.

In the writings of Nicoll and Ouspensky the instructions stress the importance of self-observation in a man's inner journey. The first thing one is told to do is to divide one's self into two—the observer and the observed. The literature of the Work stresses the fact that unless a man divides himself into two he cannot shift from where he is. But this is not enough. Help must be given in what to observe. In the Work group I was in, most of the meeting time was given to the report of members on what they had observed about themselves as they worked with the week's exercise in observation.

The exercises and instructions that follow later on are informed not only by the Work, but by religious and psychological writings. In the Work we were instructed not to pass the assignments on to others. It was a restriction that became one of the influential factors in my leaving the Work group, for my own call is to the building of the Church. Only a very few are ever authorized to teach the Work system, and then only after years of discipleship and training. It was not that Gurdjieff did not want his teachings known, but that he wanted assurance that they would not be passed on in a distorted form. Christianity might have been different had it been able to exercise a similar control, but this was never possible. The disciples were in possession of the irrepressible news, "He lives!" You simply do not tell that up and down the land and keep things in hand. Not that the Church did not try. The hierarchy of bishops and other church offices, and the painstaking selection of writings for the New Testament—these were the Church's efforts to ensure that the teachings of its Lord would not be contaminated by false doctrine.

It does not seem, however, that the failure of Christianity in our time is due to differences of interpretation. These have existed since the beginning of the Church. It lies, rather, in a pervading attitude in the Church itself that the inwardness of its life can be known without any serious commitment. It is one of those generally held illusions that we commit ourselves to something or someone on the basis of having learned all there is to know. Whereas actually, commitment is made not because we know, but in order that we may know. Neither Zen nor Yoga, Christianity nor any religion, yields its deep secrets to any but those who search with wholeness of heart, which means a heart without division.

It is possible to be a student of religions and to accumulate a vast store of interesting information, but even this only makes for conversation and does not come alive in any vital way until there is a place to apply it, and always the place where it can be applied in any significant way is at the place of one's own commitment. It has taken most of my life to discover that whatever has anything very precious to give also requires that something very precious be given in return.

Ouspensky quotes Gurdjieff as saying, "But we never give any serious secrets to a man we don't trust," and "There are things which are said only for disciples."[10] I tended at first to turn from

10. Ouspensky, op. cit., pp. 15, 14.

the esoteric sound of these words, but now I hear those same words in the Gospels, "To you the secret of the kingdom of God has been given; but to those who are outside everything comes by way of parables, so that (as Scripture says) they may look and look, but see nothing; they may hear and hear, but understand nothing. . . ."[11] The Gospels are full of passages that illustrate that Jesus gave his deeper teachings only to those who were sharing a common life with him. When the elders and chief priests and doctors addressed to him the question, "Are you the Messiah?" his answer was characteristic of his whole teaching ministry, "If I tell you, you will not believe me; and if I ask questions, you will not answer."[12] Most of his healings are followed by one of these statements: "Do not tell anyone in the village."[13] "Jesus then ordered him not to tell anybody."[14] "Then he gave them strict orders not to tell this to anyone."[15] "Jesus forbade them to tell anyone."[16] His conversation with Nicodemus is an example of how little he believed that the inwardness of the faith could be communicated in a conversation. "If you disbelieve me when I talk to you about things on earth, how are you to believe if I should talk about the things of heaven?"[17]

It was not that he was without a message for the crowds. It was simply that what he said to them was different from what he said to the committed few. He did not seem to have much faith in a man's being able to understand something just because he was told it. Even with the disciples he was slow to reveal what he knew, "There is still much that I could say to you, but the burden would be too great for you now."[18] He urged them to use the same restraint. When he asked Peter, "Who do you say I am?" and Peter answered, "God's Messiah," his immediate response was to give them strict orders not to tell anyone.[19]

I had been attending the Work meetings for several years when I

11. Mark 4:11–12 (NEB). 12. Luke 22:67–68 (NEB).
13. Mark 8:26 (NEB). 14. Luke 5:14 (NEB).
15. Luke 9:21 (NEB). 16. Mark 7:36 (NEB).
17. John 3:12 (NEB). 18. John 16:12 (NEB).
19. Luke 9:21 (NEB).

reached a plateau. I realized that I had grasped only the basic elements of what the system of ideas was about, and that there was
much more to learn and it was there for the taking, but there was
one implicit requirement. It was simply to give more of oneself than
I had time to do. I knew that if I had gone to study Zen, one day
the demand to put down one's full weight there would have been
made. Christianity has that same requirement. It also gives its secrets only to disciples. It also requires, as Kierkegaard said, that one
swim out fifty fathoms deep. Life gives to no one the time or energy
to do that in the waters of more than one ocean.

There is a time when it is right to explore many religions. One
often has to do this in order to find what grasps one at a level deep
enough to permit at least initial commitments to be made. But those
who stay merely students of religion into middle age become dreary.
They know facts and doctrines, and laws and rites, but they know
nothing of Mystery.

This does not mean that one's knowing is forever locked within
a single tradition. Not at all. Commitment gives one dialogue with
Mystery wherever it is. Thomas Merton in his fifties left his mon-
astery to travel to the East because there were men there who could
talk to him of God. A man will travel half the world for that communion, but when this is one's hunger, it is hard to go half a block
to attend a religious conference. It is one thing to listen to speeches
and have group discussions, and something quite different to share
one's journey with another who is also on a journey. In one meeting,
concepts are exchanged, and in the other, secrets.

After I left the Work meetings I did not have any new encounter
with the concept of the many selves until I met it in the book *Games
People Play* by Eric Berne. That book made a vast reading public
aware of three psychological realities each person carries in him.
Colloquially Berne described these as the Parent, the Child, and the
Adult. He writes:

These observations give rise to certain diagnostic statements. "That is
your Parent" means: "You are now in the same state of mind as one of

your parents (or a parental substitute) used to be, and you are responding as he would, with the same posture, gestures, vocabulary, feelings,
etc." "That is your Adult" means: "You have just made an autonomous,
objective appraisal of the situation and are stating these thought-processes,
or the problems you perceive, or the conclusions you have come to, in a
non-prejudicial manner." "That is your Child" means: "The manner and
intent of your reaction is the same as it would have been when you were
a very little boy or girl."[20]

This is a profound observation of psychological realities translated
into terms easily grasped by lay readers, so that they are able to use
them to observe these states in themselves and to note when the
shift is made from one to the other. I had read only the first chapter
of the book when I found myself quartered down for the night in
a hospital where I was to undergo some routine tests. My roommate
was a twenty-year-old who was there to have four wisdom teeth ex-
tracted. That afternoon she told me that this was her first time in a
hospital, but that her mother had spent many years in and out of
hospitals. She assured me that the food would be poor, the service
inadequate, and there would be little opportunity for survival if one
were not fairly well.

That evening we both had occasion to ring for the nurse. During
the half hour when she did not come, my roommate's feelings about
hospitals were confirmed and she began to say all the things she had
heard her mother say. I heard in her my own "Parent" recording
that says "hospitals are dangerous," and was able to respond by
reminding her that neither one of us was ill and that the nursing
staff was aware of that and would respond to our signal only when
those who were really ill had been taken care of. She looked at me
surprised, and then after a thoughtful pause agreed. It was as
though she had never had opportunity before to view this situation
through any eyes but those of her mother.

After that I began to listen more consciously for the "Parent"
recording in me. It was always a fresh and liberating moment when

20. Eric Berne, *Games People Play* (New York: Grove Press, 1964), p. 24.

I was able to identify one. Some recordings created division and kept me from a free, abandoned giving, for they came on at crucial moments to caution me against the foolish spending of my energies. They would say, "Let someone else do it," or "You must learn to look out for yourself." Not only had I internalized old words and played them again and again to protect the "Child" in me, but I was also responding to them with old feelings of anger and frustration. I was unable to go ahead when these records were playing, but at the same time I was unwilling to withhold myself. Old recordings may still come on at times, but the ones I have identified have lost their power to create division in me.

Now there is another book on this same theme by Thomas A. Harris: *I'm OK—You're OK*.[21] It again distinguishes those three elements, Child, Parent, and Adult in each person, and adds other dimensions. The possibilities grow that the concept of the many selves will be explored in much more depth so that we can begin to recognize not only the Child, Parent, and Adult in us, but those selves that resist being consigned to any of the three categories and demand other identities.

Freud said, in explaining atrocities committed in wartime, "When the community has no rebuke to make, there is an end of all suppression of the basic passions, and men perpetrate deeds of cruelty, fraud, treachery and barbarity so incompatible with their civilization that one would have held them to be impossible."[22] If we needed from our own day any confirmation of this statement we have seen it in the massacre at My Lai in Vietnam. Freud explains this kind of event by saying that every earlier stage of development persists alongside the later stage which has developed from it. The primitive mind is imperishable and can be re-established. It would seem to be an accurate restatement of the same proposition to say that in each of us is a primitive or savage who is ready to cast off

21. New York: Harper & Row, 1969.
22. Sigmund Freud, *On Creativity and the Unconscious* (New York: Harper Torchbook, 1958), p. 212.

any veneer of civilization. When feelings of anger, frustration, hate, and fear run deep, we can recognize, if we can begin to look, the primitive that stalks one's own life. Child or Adult or Parent hardly describes this one, who is of earth and cave.

There are helpful aids in identifying the many selves. We see them in the different roles we play—parent, sister, worker, expert, servant, organizer, creator—there are myriad roles we take on ourselves, and then there are the roles that others give us, which we obediently and all unconsciously play out for them. Almost everyone has had the experience of having one person evoke what is negative in him while another calls forth a loving and confirming self. When we begin to have some understanding of our many selves, we begin to see how much things outside of us—persons and situations and circumstances—determine what part of us is in ascendancy and how a life that has not found its center is "at the mercy of every chance wind of teaching and the jockeying of men. . . ."[23]

Conversely, we may consistently pull from a person a negative self and find it difficult to comprehend why others fail to see in that person what is so distressing to us. If things do not go well for us, we have difficulty in understanding that we have any part in creating the response we are receiving or the atmosphere in which we find ourselves. We reflect on the situation with that self which hungers for harmony and relationship and are unaware of the negative self that evokes negative responses.

It is possible to act out our whole lives in what Bruce Evans, minister of The Fellowship Church in Baton Rouge, Louisiana, has called "roles of lostness." He identifies one primary role as that of "god" and another that of "baby." They seem to lie at opposite poles, but are probably very closely related, for it is not uncommon for the baby self to take over when the god self gets in difficulty. There is a striking example of this in the story of King Ahab, who coveted the vineyard of his neighbor, Naboth.[24] In his god role Ahab in-

23. Eph. 4:14 (Phillips).   24. 1 Kings 21.

dulged all his wishes. It was his to ask and for others to obey, and so he proposed that Naboth sell him his vineyard to be used for a palace garden. But Naboth had in him a self with a strong sense of the historical and was outraged by the suggestion. He replied, "The Lord forbid that I should let you have land which has always been in my family."[25] At the refusal of Naboth to sell his land, the king-god reverted to the state of baby: "He lay down on his bed, covered his face and refused to eat." How different might have been the story of murder that followed, if Ahab could have separated from these selves—stood off from them and inquired of the god self the reason for its covetousness, and of the baby self the reason for its anger. These were controlling and immobilizing feelings in Ahab. If he had attended to them, they would have put him in touch with unknown parts of himself. As it was, he was their victim and their tool. The god self and the baby self still determine not only the history of our own households but the history of nations.

The place of temptation is also excellent ground from which to view the division in us. Here rages the conflict between the good guys and the bad guys. In biblical terms it is described as the war between our lower and higher natures, or light and darkness, or heaven and earth. The writer of Galatians gave this advice.

Live your whole life in the Spirit and you will not satisfy the desires of your lower nature. For the whole energy of the lower nature is set against the Spirit, while the whole power of the Spirit is contrary to the lower nature. Here is the conflict, and that is why you are not free to do what you want to do. But if you follow the leading of the Spirit, you stand clear of the Law.[26]

But that counsel is for those who are old in the faith. Paul speaks more for some of us when he describes a feeling of helplessness.

I do not understand my own actions. For I do not do what I want, but I do the very thing I hate. . . . For I delight in the law of God, in my inmost self, but I see in my members another law at war with the law of

25. 1 Kings 21:3 (NEB).   26. Gal. 5:16 (Phillips).

my mind and making me captive to the law of sin which dwells in my members.[27]

The conflict between our different I's is also easily observed in the resolutions we make and cannot follow. Most of us have an I which will tell us to postpone to another time any course of action we resolve to follow. Often where resolutions are being made we have selves whose very existence is being threatened. They will deceive and lie and argue their case with eloquent logic. But as with all selves that are closely observed, their words tend to grow stale and hackneyed and some of the power goes out of them.

Several years ago at a retreat for women who wanted to lose weight we used the method of observing the different selves to try to understand some of the inner dynamics of the weight problem, and to become familiar with the territory on which the real battle would be waged.

Participants in this retreat were asked to ponder during the semifast days of the retreat the following questions:

What I's in me want to eat?
　　What is the aim of each of these I's?
　　What does each fear?
　　What is the speech that each makes?
What I's do not want to eat?
　　What are their aims?
　　What are their fears?
　　What is the speech that each makes?

It proved an excellent way to be in dialogue with the many selves that will spring to life in us whenever we make a resolution.

At any crossroads where decision is called for, we may also be able to discern the many selves. If we will take time to reflect on some of the turning points in our lives, we can get a fairly good picture of the influences that have been dominating our internal establishment. A power struggle has gone on there too, and there

27. Rom. 7:15, 22–23 (RSV).

may be a hierarchy of selves in power keeping that ideal self which each of us cherishes from ever coming into its own. I have a friend who considered the turning points in his life and said, "I always took the way of least resistance and of least challenge. It has filled me with discontent because something in me knew something else and wanted it." Unless the real self gets nurtured and strikes its roots in something deep, it will be pushed out of the way by negative selves that often operate outside of consciousness and resist being identified, for there is a psychological law that what is named can be controlled.

It is precisely because the application of the concept of the many selves helps with the "naming" that it offers new possibilities for self-understanding. As it is now, we see ourselves as one. If we identify with a lovely, gracious self, then we will tend to resist any knowledge that threatens that image. If it is a dark self we are identified with, our light components are cast into outer darkness, which is to say into unconsciousness. Whereas if we understood our plurality we would not be so menaced by the possibility of being swallowed up by any one of our many selves. The recognition that we are more than one person allows us not only to better identify various aspects of ourselves, but to gain the objectivity or distance that is needed to be in real communication with them. It is not unlike the psychological space that is needed in our relationship with others if we are to have any meaningful encounter.

Either experientially or intellectually we have a grasp of what it means for a person to lose his identity in another person, so that he is absorbed by that person and exists in that person, and even says, "I cannot live without him." Growing up is establishing one's separateness from parents. But with our children the separateness must be established again. We must free them to develop apart from us, which means that we must free them without making them feel anxious. That is not possible when we experience them as extensions of ourselves whose going will grievously wound us—maybe unto death. To the degree that we invest any person with the ultimate meaning of our life we will put on that person demands he cannot possibly fulfill. It often remains a lifetime relationship of disappointment and hurt. If the separation between parent and child is not successfully made, then part of us will continue to operate out of that stage of our history. The child in us who refused to grow up will find in almost every situation someone who can be cast as the father or mother and is willing to play the part, for there is always someone around who has a self which is in search of a child or a disciple. In some of these relationships no effort is made to communicate, since the assumption is that the other person as the all-knowing parent or dutiful child will know what is going on in our thoughts and feelings. Much of our hurt comes not only because the other person fails to give us what we need, but because we have cast him in the parent or god role, and it is assumed that he knows what we lack without being told.

"Ask, and you will receive"[28] needs to be given to congregations to practice on a human level. "I was sick and nobody came to see me" or a similar complaint is heard in a hundred situations. Where one is emotionally dependent or so merged with another that there is not enough experience of separateness, it is difficult to see the need for letting that person know what one feels or thinks. Since "we think and feel as one" (it is assumed), the other "already knows." This identification can be mistaken for love. The logic then is, "If you loved me, you would know what I need. I would not have to ask." There is here no recognition of the responsibility that each of us has to struggle to communicate his feelings and needs; nor is there respect for the fact that another may have other claims upon his attention or even hurt feelings of his own to deal with. It accounts for some seemingly violent disruptions in what appear like perfect relationships, and of course manifests itself in less extreme forms at other points. It may explain the often consistent failure of some persons to choose gifts which give enjoyment to others. They do not see the uniqueness of the other and feel that in satisfying their own tastes they will surely give pleasure.

28. Matt. 7:7 (NEB).

It is especially difficult to gain separateness from significant persons and groups when we fear the choosing of a different direction or the development of different opinions will cut us off from acceptance. This is equally true of one's attitude toward nation and culture and times. "My country," "my life-style," or "my generation" may indicate such strong identification with one's group that there is no real exchange within the group, let alone beyond it, with other countries, cultures, and generations. The capacity to transcend their generation's culture and mind-set is what made the discoveries of Copernicus and Darwin and Freud more than the discoveries of genius. All three had to overcome "dread of the community," for their discoveries were to strike hard at some of man's cherished illusions. In the realm of the spirit their heroism singled them out as giants among men. Fear of losing the acceptance of those to whom we belong will turn the most intrepid of us from the path of self-discovery as well as discovery that might threaten the external orders in which we live. We can hold all unconsciously the powerful fear that if we were really to discover our feelings and direction, they would lead us away from the persons and groups that give us meaning and belonging. Or the fear may be that the discovery of our separate ways will evoke in others the hostility that will make them turn from us. When the Church talks about finding identity in a transcendent order—"the life I now live is not my life, but the life which Christ lives in me"[29]—it is talking about a rootedness for one's being which creates the space between men that enables them to see each other and not be threatened by differences, but to be celebrators of mystery in one another.

The separateness, or space, or distance that we need between persons in the external orders of our lives, so that there can be genuine community in which we are truly members of one another, must first be achieved in our internal households. It is here that Christian detachment begins. If I identify with an opinion, or feeling, or mood, I do not have the distance I need to examine it and to

29. Gal. 2:20 (NEB).

find out how representative it is of the whole of me, and how much
power I want to give it to determine the direction of my life. I am
literally in bondage. In tone and movement, if not in words, my
feelings say, "This is my opinion. If you reject my opinion, you
reject me. We are one and the same." Or I pronounce, as Ahab did,
"I must have this vineyard. I am consumed by my desire. It makes
everything else unimportant."

Ananias and Sapphira are an interesting study of divided persons
who were literally destroyed by feelings they did not understand.[30]
Their story, however, can make us uncomfortable, for it is hard to
keep it in a clinical setting. If we look long enough, they are apt to
become mirrors in which we see our own disease. They were
obviously fearful people who wanted very much to belong to the
community that was springing up around them. Their problem was
that it had been catapulted into a style of life for which neither
Ananias nor his wife was ready. They wanted it, and were afraid
of it. They could not bear to leave it, but neither could they wholly
commit themselves.

A reckless abandon characterized the community. No one in it
said that "any of the things which he possessed was his own, but
they had everything in common."[31] More than that, those who did
have property were selling it and giving the proceeds to the disciples, who were free to distribute them to anyone in need. It is a
terrifying thing to give up the rewards of all the years of your labor,
when you have a self in you that is disbelieving—one for whom
those possessions represent safety and a known future, one that
makes little speeches like, "Can you really trust them?" "When you
are sick and can't work any longer, who will take care of you then?"

Perhaps there were yet other selves that dreaded involvement,
that wanted to be free to come and go and could not face being
forever bound. I feel that I know the state they were in, because I
too live in a community that occasionally gets drenched with the
Spirit. It is then that some of us know the struggle of the many

30. Acts 5.   31. Acts 4:32 (RSV).

selves, for is there anyone who does not have inside an Ananias or a Sapphira? There is still no descent of the Spirit with its unifying action unless we can encounter our own withholding self. Wherever there is a community of acceptance this is more possible.

Perhaps there was acceptance in that first Christian community and Ananias and Sapphira simply did not belong enough to know it. In any event they were not able to confess their reservations. The fateful plan they hit upon was to give each of their conflicting selves a voice in their decision. As we know, they sold a piece of property and agreed together that they would hand over only a part of the proceeds to the apostles, while making it appear to the onlooking community that they were giving the whole amount.

The tragic story reads that Peter confronted each separately with the knowledge that no one was deceived. The belonging, the security, the opportunity to be persons in community which they so sorely needed and for which they had so innocently sacrificed integrity, seemed in that moment of confrontation to be utterly lost. The disclosure of the lying part of themselves to a community they had not fully learned to trust was literally more than each could bear. Their falling dead was a drastic fulfillment of Scripture that appears in many forms in the Old and New Testaments. "No city or house divided against itself will stand"[32] is a severe warning, as are the words of Hosea, "Their heart is divided: Now shall they perish."[33] Meister Eckhart explains it by saying that "division by its very nature is the way to non-being (non esse)—division by its very nature is privation and nothing—no thing."[34]

It is important to note that the community had not demanded the property of them. This is made clear in Peter's statement, "While it remained unsold, did it not remain your own? And after it was sold, was it not at your disposal?"[35] What they could not believe was that they would be fully accepted, if it was known that the

32. Matt. 12:25 (RSV).   33. Hos. 10:2.
34. Meister Eckhart, *Treatises and Sermons,* James M. Clark and John V. Skinner, sel. and trans. (New York: Harper & Row, 1958), p. 218.
35. Acts 5:4 (RSV).

Spirit that was moving in the community had not yet touched a crucial dimension of their lives. They feared that if they admitted they were not yet ready to take the step of giving all they owned they would be judged and found wanting. I have a feeling that it is these same fears that have alienated modern man from himself and made it impossible for him to be a person on pilgrimage. We so long for the approval of others that we have pretended to be what we are not.

Despite the teachings of psychoanalytical literature, which have given us an intellectual understanding of the importance of recognizing our negative feelings if they are not to control us, most of the people I meet in small groups do not seem to feel that this is their need. They are tired of the Christian Church's emphasis on darkness and denial and hold it in part responsible for their own feelings of low self-esteem. The cry today is for the attention to be on creativity and gifts and self-worth and play. There is strong resistance to anything that would go back to the old. The glimmer we have from time to time of the meaning and significance of confession is in danger of flickering out, if we do not get hold of a deeper understanding of how intricately our darkness is bound up with our light. No one is going to have a dancing life or a soul that walks in anything but worn-out shoes unless we make some fateful connection with our own evil.

And yet, there is something authentic in the feeling that one is a betrayer of self when one says, "I am jealous," "I am envious," or "I am greedy," and something authentic in the fear that this will evoke a judgmental attitude in others, especially in those who have not identified these qualities in themselves. No one of these feelings is ever representative of the whole of a person. Ananias and Sapphira had parts of them which did hold back, but there was also an ache in them to belong to this community that was giving its testimony to the new creation. They would not have been so strongly attracted if parts of them had not yearned for the hearing of that Word. The resisting, fearful selves needed to be raised into consciousness for them to know the power of the Resurrection, but they shrank from this, and somehow it seems understandable. If I say, "I am jealous," it describes the whole of me, and I am overwhelmed with its implications. The completeness of the statement makes me feel contemptuous of myself. It is little wonder that I fear letting another know when my own identity with the feeling is such that it describes the totality of who I am. But suppose that each of us understood the multiplicity of his life. What if it were such common knowledge that only an ignorant person would ever be heard to say, "Well, if he is that way, I want nothing to do with him," as though the "way" of a person could be known just because one of his selves was glimpsed for a moment.

If I respect the plurality in myself, and no longer see my jealous self as the whole of me, then I have gained the distance I need to observe it, listen to it, and let it acquaint me with a piece of my own lost history. In this way I come into possession of more of myself and extend my own inner kingdom. Suppose we come to know that every recognition of anger and jealousy and greed and sloth is an opportunity to lift out of the waters of unconsciousness a tiny piece of submerged land. Then, would we not pity the man who is so identified with the good that he denies any intimations from below that this good may not be the whole of him? Such a man is lost. Unaware that he is cut off from a large part of himself, he does not understand what it means to be on the journey of becoming whole.

Our praise is partial praise, our response is a partial response, our love partial love. We must find our own lost territories and fulfill the command to make them His disciples, baptizing them in the name of the Father and the Son and the Holy Spirit.

Go forth therefore and make all nations my disciples; baptize men everywhere in the name of the Father and the Son and the Holy Spirit, and teach them to observe all that I have commanded you.[36]

It is true, of course, that not everyone has a jealous self that causes him as much torment as the jealous self he sees in his neighbor. But then it is well to look for the tyranny of a greedy self or a lazy

36. Matt. 28:19-20 (NEB).

one. I once took a beginner's class in Yoga exercises in which the teacher always chose the most apt pupil to illustrate the different positions. A student with no practice could illustrate the perfect cobra hold, but this would not be the student who could illustrate the bow. Often when a student had performed well, the instructor would say to the rest of us, "Do not be envious. There will be something she cannot do." And it would always happen that way. The person who was best able to execute one posture had the most to learn in the performance of another. This is the way it is in life. In one area we will have little to learn and in another very much.

The concept of the many selves gives the detachment and distance that we need to name and understand all the happenings in us. It is a simple handle for identifying the contradictions and ambivalences that Scripture and Dostoevsky and Freud talk to us about in other terms. With it we can stand back and get the distance we need in order to see the division and multiplicity in our own inner worlds. Christianity does not talk very much these days about detachment, and it is probably well that it doesn't. It is useless to talk to people about becoming detached from possessions and persons if they have no help in becoming detached from their own "society of selves." It is the poverty of this inner community that produces the driving desire to have and to get.

Multiplicity and division can probably be best understood in terms of their opposites: oneness and unity. When it was said of Ananias and Sapphira that they were willing to sacrifice their integrity, this was saying that they were willing to sacrifice the state of being complete or unbroken. This is the dictionary definition of integrity. It is a state of purity. No wonder that Kierkegaard made the refrain of a book, "Purity of heart is to will one thing."

So much of our real suffering comes because there is no integration of our many selves around the Self which is "in the Lord." Unity, however, can be achieved around other selves. It is not unusual for a person to have a large part of himself integrated around a lying self. This kind of integration could be shattered, if the truth grew strong in other parts. It seems important to say this, since not

all breaking up is evil. Often it is an opportunity to get back together around a new center. There would be no possibility for
completeness or wholeness if too many of our selves were integrated
around the child in us. That kind of integration can force us to live
our whole lives captive to the role of baby, with the cry, "Please take
care of me—I am helpless and cannot take care of myself."

Everyone has had some experience with the suffering this kind of
dependence produces. It is to be hoped that other selves in us will
grow strong enough to throw the whole internal order into conflict,
so that the gathering in can be around new values and truths. The
pain of growth that is talked about so much is often this breaking
up of the old. I resist, however, speaking of this kind of growth
as pain, because it has always seemed to me that it is not to be
compared with the terrible pain of staying integrated around lies
or some earlier stage that does not belong to the present period of
one's history.

When we are integrated around the negative selves, we feel inferior, less than human. We are out of touch with those selves that
could bridge a thousand chasms. But when we are identified with
only the good in us, we exclude from integration the objectionable.
It is kept out of consciousness and cut off from acceptance.

Though at first glance it may seem a better situation to be identified with good than with evil, there is a time to "not resist one
who is evil."[37] What we repress in ourselves, we will project onto
the neighbor and try to destroy there. The old ethic said that the
way to deal with these negative selves was by annihilation. We
stamped on them and forbade them to make themselves known.
Evil, we said, is evil. It cannot be allowed to exist. Wipe it out! In
the psychic world this meant to wipe it out of consciousness. We
now know that this is not possible and that the way to handle even
evil is first to take it in one's embrace. This is how it is transformed
and integrated into the whole; or, this is how exorcism takes place.
The children of dark love the dark, and simply by being delivered
into the light of consciousness they are sometimes cast out forever.

37. Matt. 5:39 (RSV).

There are, however, other shadow selves that do not give up like this. They resist having their energies redirected. Until the process of redemption occurs we are to love even these selves. The chances are that we have not heard them out and that they have much to tell us about unknown parts of ourselves that cry to be born. Does my envy of the artist tell me of the sleeping creator in my own being? Does my covetousness of my friend's children tell the childless me that I have a self that needs to find the motherless to mother? Does my greed, if I will accept and listen to it, direct me to the task of tending to my inner poverty? My very wholeness may depend on my willingness to keep company with these strange dark messengers.

Then there are those selves which will serve us well when assigned to their proper places in the internal establishment. If he is not known, the child in us will appear at inappropriate times and wreak havoc, but how would any of us fare without that child? Not only does he come to acquaint us with some of the ruins of our own antiquity, but as Harris reminds us, in this child reside also delight and play and creativity—"the countless, grand, *a-ha* experiences."[38]

But if you protest, "There is a self which is evil and tells me nothing, and destroys where I would build," the answer is still to love that self. The message is that this self is also redeemable.

Probably no one in this century has given more attention to the subject of evil than Martin Buber. Maurice Friedman, his able translator and eloquent interpreter, has said that although significant changes occurred in Buber's thought during fifty years of productivity, he never lost his faith in the redemption of evil. Friedman writes:

Elizabeth Rotten has quoted Buber as saying, "One must also love evil . . . even as evil wishes to be loved." This statement is symbolic of the way in which he has consistently answered this question: good can be maximized not through the rejection or conquest of evil but only through

38. Op. cit., p. 27.

the transformation of evil, the use of its energy and passion in the service of the good.[39]

The Spirit which is the Spirit of Truth will guide us into our truth, if we will ask. That Spirit will create unity within us so that all the selves are under the one Self which is grounded in the one God. When the unifying work of the Spirit goes on, more and more of the unconscious is restored to consciousness, and we move toward the fulfillment of the command to love God with the whole of us. We begin to find union with Him, that rest toward which our restlessness directs us. By the action of the Godhead—the three persons in One—all the persons in us are centered in the One. To know peace where there was conflict, to know unity where there was multiplicity, to be the "single one" instead of the "double-minded" is to have the feel of the new creation and to receive the second commandment, "and love thy neighbor as thyself."

The neighbor is also divided. In him also is multiplicity. He, too, suffers the pain of his division. He is more than the angry or violent one who wants his hour on the stage. He also has one who holds back and one who loves the Lord and presses toward the company of those who have the words of the Resurrection. In our neighbor we find our own humanity.

It is written of St. Francis that he got down off his horse and embraced the leper. Will I do the same for the lost one I meet on the streets of my own life, and will I do the same for the lost one I meet on the streets of the world? Of all the questions that are raised by the anguish of the days in which we live, this is the question I find addressed to me.

39. *Martin Buber: The Life of Dialogue* (New York: Harper Torchbook, 1955), p. 15.

EXERCISE 1

Observe your different selves

Try to observe the different selves in you. You might list in your journal the roles you have in life, and during the week try to observe the different selves that are called into existence by each of these roles.

Another way to work on the exercise is to try to identify the Child, Parent, and Adult in you.

What are the selves that you cherish and would like to strengthen? What are the ones you dislike?

In your time of meditation, reflect on your many selves. Do you control them all or are there some that spring uninvited onto the stage of your life and refuse direction? As help in working on this assignment, each day choose a few of the following selections for meditative reading. Against the backdrop of what you read, consider your own life.

I have too many selves to know the one.
In too complex a schooling was I bred,
Child of too many cities, who have gone
Down all bright cross-roads of the world's desires,
And at too many altars bowed my head
To light too many fires.
    —"A Plaint of Complexity" by Eunice Tietjens,
                    The Dial, May 31, 1919

EVERYBODY has his own theatre, in which he is manager, actor, prompter, playwright, sceneshifter, boxkeeper, doorkeeper, all in one, and audience into the bargain.
    —Julius Charles Hare and Augustus William Hare, *Guesses at Truth,* Series 2 (*Oxford Dictionary of Quotations,* p. 237)

"I DO not have much success in my inner work. No sooner do I step out of the door, or arrive at the office, or have a difficult interview or some crisis to cope with than all my inner resolves are forgotten. I lose my way. I react mechanically. I become a slave. I am pushed around by my impressions. Events take charge and my inner aim disappears. Some external aim takes its place. I become a different person."

Sincere observation soon brings the student face to face with this fact. There is no single self. A man is one self at home and another at the office; one self at work, another when on vacation; one self with his wife, another with his secretary. Now and then, after some lapse of behavior, he may express astonishment or regret: "I don't know what possessed me. That is not the real me, I forgot myself." To which the careful investigator will reply, "Forgot which self?" For it should be fairly obvious from the above that *multiplicity of selves is the common condition.* Existence of a single "I" corresponding to a single aim and a single will is the exception rather than the rule.

.   .   .   .   .

For an enlightened study of the selves, two attitudes are necessary: acceptance of their multiplicity and acceptance of their me-
chanicalness. The selves are like a box of clockwork dolls, some
dressed one way, some another, some pleasant, some unpleasant,
some clever, some stupid. The dolls have no free will. They are
wound up and activated by circumstances. Under a given set of
conditions, one of the dolls will leave the box, go through its
performance, lapse back into quiescence. . . . It is the task of the
Observer, that element of man's being which carries within it the
seed of higher consciousness, to watch the puppets, learn how they
behave, gradually accumulate material concerning their roles. To do
this he must learn to be impartial. He will never obtain an understanding of the contents of his box of dolls if he refuses to look
at *all of them,* the ugly, misshapen, villainous ones as well as those
which seem pretty. This calls for effort and honesty as well as
accurate observation.

—Robert S. De Ropp, *The Master Game,* pp. 93, 101

NOVEMBER 29, 1968. For Zorba With Love

Zorba, forever on my mind. I curse and love you because I am what
I am. You hold up a mirror to my sometimes too serious face. Like
the boss, I think too much. But there is often dancing in my mind,
ideas frolicking. Sometimes my body is moved. Yet I am a careful
person, taking thought for the morrow. I don't know how to care
without being careful, without remaining faithful to the "full catas-
trophe" of rootedness in a profession and a family.

But I long to release the gypsy in me who would roam the earth,
tasting, sampling, traveling light. There are so many lives I want
to live, so many styles I want to inhabit. In me sleeps Zorba's
concern to allow no lonely woman to remain comfortless. (Here am
I, Lord—send me!) Camus's passion to lessen the suffering of the
innocent. Hemingway's drive to live and write with lucidity, and
the unheroic desire to see each day end with tranquillity and a
shared cup of tea.

I am so many, yet I may only be one. I mourn for all the selves
I kill when I decide to be a single person. Decision is a cutting off,

castration. I travel one path only by neglecting many. Actual existence is tragic, but fantastic existence (which evades choice and
limitation) is pathetic. The human choice may be between tragedy
and pathos, Oedipus and Willy Loman. So I turn my back on small
villages I will never see, strange flesh I will not touch, ills I will
not cure, and I choose to be in the world as a husband, a father, an
explorer of ideas and styles of life. Perhaps Zorba will not leave
me altogether. I would not like to live without dancing, without
unknown roads to explore, without the confidence that my actions
were helpful to some.

        —Sam Keen, *To a Dancing God,* pp. 119–120

WHEN a village grows into a town or a child into a man, the village
and the child become lost in the town and the man. Memory alone
can trace the old features in the new picture; and in fact the old
materials or forms have been got rid of and replaced by new ones.
It is otherwise with the development of the mind. Here one can
describe the state of affairs, which has nothing to compare with it,
only by saying that in this case every earlier stage of development
persists alongside the later stage which has arisen from it; here
succession also involves co-existence, although it is to the same
materials that the whole series of transformations has applied. The
earlier mental state may not have manifested itself for years, but
none the less it is so far present that it may at any time again become the mode of expression of the forces in the mind, and indeed
the only one, as though all later developments had been annulled
or undone. This extraordinary plasticity of mental developments is
not unrestricted as regards direction; it may be described as a special
capacity for involution—for regression—since it may well happen
that a later and higher stage of development, once abandoned, cannot be reached again. But the primitive stages can always be re-
established; the primitive mind is, in the fullest meaning of the
word, imperishable.

        —Sigmund Freud, *Complete Psychological Works,* Vol. XIV,
                            pp. 285–286

WHAT will forever separate Freud's way from that of other psychoanalysts . . . is that his discoveries were made by himself. They were the triumph of a mind in search of itself, which, in reaching its aims, discovered the laws governing the emotional processes of all minds. We learn these discoveries with the help of books and lectures, we make them again, rediscover them when we are in the process of analysis—that is, when we are analyzed or when we analyze others. Our psychoanalytic institutes seem to be unaware of the fact that being analyzed cannot compete in experience value with unearthing these insights oneself. The one experience cannot be likened to the other. . . . One's own psychoanalysis—however important, indeed indispensable, for the understanding of oneself and others—is, of course, not comparable to the process by which Freud arrived at his results by a heroic mental deed, by a victory over his own inner reluctances and resistances. When we are analyzed by others, it is an entirely different process, induced from outside even when we ask for it ourselves. It lacks the intimacy and the depth of experience felt in discovering one's secrets oneself. Nothing said to us, nothing we can learn from others, reaches us so deep as that which we find in ourselves.

—Theodore Reik, *The Search Within,* p. 263

AT ANY GIVEN MOMENT each individual in a social aggregation will exhibit a Parental, Adult or Child ego state, and that individual can shift with varying degrees of readiness from one ego state to another. These observations give rise to certain diagnostic statements. "That is your Parent" means: "You are now in the same state of mind as one of your parents (or a parental substitute) used to be, and you are responding as he would, with the same posture, gestures, vocabulary, feelings, etc." "That is your Adult" means: "You have just made an autonomous, objective appraisal of the situation and are stating these thought-processes, or the problems you perceive, or the conclusions you have come to, in a nonprejudicial manner." "That is your Child" means: "The manner and intent of your reaction is the same as it would have been when you were a very little boy or girl."

.   .   .   .   .

ALL THREE ASPECTS of the personality have a high survival and living value, and it is only when one or the other of them disturbs the healthy balance that analysis and reorganization are indicated. Otherwise each of them, Parent, Adult, and Child, is entitled to equal respect and has its legitimate place in a full and productive life.

—Eric Berne, *Games People Play*, pp. 24, 27

A THIRD CLUE to the meaning and origin of conflict is familiar to us under the cliché, "conflict of the generations." Like the two sexes, the generations also live within ourselves. The child within is a very real factor to be dealt with, both as a backward-harking infantilism and as a developing potential in ourselves. So also a wise older self is there in outline long before we reach old age. These and all the seven ages of man we can and do project on to our children, siblings, parents, and friends, and untold conflicts arise therefrom. As each new phase rises above the horizon of our consciousness, its dawn is heralded by feelings of fascination and fear: fascination because it is so intimately ours and we need it like water in the desert or air in a caved-in mine, fear because it is the Unknown and the task of tracing its outlines seems as hard as identifying a landscape from an airplane at night, with one's life depending on it.

—Elined Prys Kotschnig, "Creative Conflict," *Inward Light,*
No. 39

TO TAKE another person as one and the same person at all times, to suppose he is one single "I", is to do violence to him and in the same way is to do violence to oneself. A multitude of different people live in each of you. These are all the different "I"'s belonging to personality, which it is necessary to observe, and try to get to know, otherwise no *self-knowledge* is possible—that is, if one really seeks *self-knowledge* and not invention and imagination about one-self. Not one of you here has a real permanent, unchanging "I". Not one of you here has a real unity of being. All of you are nothing but a crowd of different people, some better and some worse, and each of these people—each of these "I"s in you—at particular moments takes charge of you and makes you do what it wants and say what it wishes and feel and think as it feels and thinks.

.   .   .   .   .

When a man begins to observe himself from the angle that he is not one but many, he begins to work on his being. He cannot do this if he remains under the conviction that he is one, for then he will not be able to separate himself from himself, for he will take everything in him, every thought, mood, feeling, impulse, desire, emotion, and so on, as himself—that is, as "I". But if he begins to observe himself, he will then at that moment, become two—an observing side and an observed side.

.   .   .   .   .

A day in one's life is a small replica of one's life. If a man does not work on a day in his life, he cannot change his life, and if he says that he wishes to work on his life and change it, and does not work on a day in his life, his work on himself remains purely imaginary. He solaces himself with the imagination that he is going to work on his life and actually never begins to work on a single day of his life. One's life is broken up into days and years. If a man does not work on a day of his life . . . there is no starting point.

— Maurice Nicoll, *Psychological Commentaries,* Vol. 1,
pp. 20, 21, 25

SONG TO MY OTHER SELF

Over the years I have caught glimpses of you
in the mirror, wicked;
in a sudden stridency in my own voice, have
heard you mock me;

in the tightening of my muscles felt the pull
of your anger and the whine
of your greed twist my countenance; felt your
indifference blank my face when pity was called for.
You are there, lurking under every kind act I do,
ready to defeat me.
Lately, rather than drop the lid of my shock
over your intrusion,
I have looked for you with new eyes
opened to your tricks, but more,
opened to your rootedness in life.
Come, I open my arms to you also, once-dread stranger.
Come, as a friend I would welcome you to stretch your
     apartments
within me from the cramped to comforting side.
Thus I would disarm you. For I have recently learned,
learned looking straight into your eyes:
The holiness of God is everywhere.
                    —Elsie Landstrom, *Inward Light,* No. 67

VERY OFTEN, almost at every talk, G.[40] returned to the absence of
unity in man. . . .

"Man has no individuality. He has no single, big I. Man is divided into a multiplicity of small I's.

"And each separate small I is able to call itself by the name of
the Whole, to act in the name of the Whole, to agree or disagree,
to give promises, to make decisions, with which another I or the
Whole will have to deal. This explains why people so often make
decisions and so seldom carry them out. A man decides to get up
early beginning from the following day. One I, or a group of I's,
decide this. But getting up is the business of another I who entirely
disagrees with the decision and may even know absolutely nothing

40. Georges Gurdjieff.

about it. Of course the man will again go on sleeping in the morning and in the evening he will again decide to get up early. In some
cases this may assume very unpleasant consequences for a man. A
small accidental I may promise something, not to itself, but to
someone else at a certain moment simply out of vanity or for amusement. Then it disappears, but the man, that is, the whole combination of other I's who are quite innocent of this, may have to pay
for it all his life. It is the tragedy of the human being that any small
I has the right to sign checks and promissory notes and the man,
that is, the Whole has to meet them. People's whole lives often
consist in paying off the promissory notes of small accidental I's.

"Eastern teachings contain various allegorical pictures which
endeavor to portray the nature of man's being from this point of
view.

"Thus, in one teaching, man is compared to a house in which
there is a multitude of servants but no master and no steward. The
servants have all forgotten their duties; no one wants to do what he
ought; everyone tries to be master, if only for a moment; and, in
this kind of disorder, the house is threatened with grave danger.
The only chance of salvation is for a group of the more sensible
servants to meet together and elect a *temporary* steward, that is, a
deputy steward. This *deputy steward* can then put the other servants
in their places, and make each do his own work: the cook in the
kitchen, the coachman in the stables, the gardener in the garden,
and so on. In this way the 'house' can be got ready for the arrival of
the real steward who will, in his turn, prepare it for the arrival of
the master.

"The comparison of a man to a house awaiting the arrival of the
master is frequently met with in Eastern teachings which have preserved traces of ancient knowledge, and, as we know, the subject
appears under various forms in many of the parables in the Gospels.

"But even the clearest understanding of his possibilities will not
bring man any nearer to their realization. In order to realize these
possibilities he must have a very strong desire for liberation and be

willing to sacrifice everything, to risk everything, for the sake of
this liberation."

—P. D. Ouspensky, *In Search of the Miraculous*, pp. 59–61

WHO AM I?

Who am I? They often tell me
I stepped from my cell's confinement
Calmly, cheerfully, firmly,
Like a squire from his country-house.
Who am I? They often tell me
I used to speak to my warders
Freely and friendly and clearly,
As though it were mine to command.
Who am I? They also tell me
I bore the days of misfortune
Equably, smilingly, proudly,
Like one accustomed to win.

Am I then really all that which other men tell of?
Or am I only what I myself know of myself?
Restless and longing and sick, like a bird in a cage,
Struggling for breath, as though hands were compressing
    my throat,
Yearning for colours, for flowers, for the voices of birds,
Thirsting for words of kindness, for neighbourliness,
Tossing in expectation of great events,
Powerlessly trembling for friends at infinite distance,
Weary and empty at praying, at thinking, at making,
Faint, and ready to say farewell to it all?

Who am I? This or the other?
Am I one person to-day and to-morrow another?
Am I both at once? A hypocrite before others,

And before myself a contemptibly woebegone weakling?
Or is something within me still like a beaten army,
Fleeing in disorder from victory already achieved?

Who am I? They mock me, these lonely questions of mine.
Whoever I am, Thou knowest, O God, I am Thine!
          —Dietrich Bonhoeffer, *Letters and Papers from Prison,*
                                        pp. 221–222

WE WESTERN PEOPLES are apt to think our great problems are external, environmental. We are not skilled in the inner life, where
the real roots of our problem lie. For I would suggest that the true
explanation of the complexity of our program is an inner one,
not an outer one. The outer distractions of our interests reflect an
inner lack of integration of our own lives. We are trying to be
several selves at once, without all our selves being organized by a
single, mastering Life within us. Each of us tends to be, not a single
self, but a whole committee of selves. There is the civic self, the
parental self, the financial self, the religious self, the society self,
the professional self, the literary self. And each of our selves is in
turn a rank individualist, not cooperative but shouting out his vote
loudly for himself when the voting time comes. And all too com-
monly we follow the common American method of getting a quick
decision among conflicting claims within us. It is as if we have a
chairman of our committee of the many selves within us, who does
not integrate the many into one but who merely counts the votes
at each decision, and leaves disgruntled minorities. The claims of
each self are still pressed. If we accept service on a committee on
Negro education, we still regret we can't help with a Sunday-school
class. We are not integrated. We are distraught. We feel honestly
the pull of many obligations and try to fulfill them all.

                    .   .   .   .   .

Life is meant to be lived from a Center, a divine Center. Each one
of us can live such a life of amazing power and peace and serenity,

of integration and confidence and simplified multiplicity, on one condition—that is, *if we really want to*. There is a divine Abyss within us all, a holy Infinite Center, a Heart, a Life who speaks in us and through us to the world. We have all heard this holy Whisper at times. At times we have followed the Whisper, and amazing equilibrium of life, amazing effectiveness of living set in. But too many of us have heeded the Voice only at times. Only at times have we submitted to His holy guidance. We have not counted this Holy Thing within us to be the most precious thing in the world. We have not surrendered *all else,* to attend to it alone. . . .

John Woolman did. He resolved so to order his outward affairs as to be, *at every moment,* attentive to that voice. . . .

. . . He didn't have to struggle, and renounce, and strain to achieve simplicity. He yielded to the Center and his life became simple. It was synoptic. It had singleness of eye. "If thine eye be single thy whole body shall be full of light." His many selves were integrated into a single true self, whose whole aim was humbly walking in the presence and guidance and will of God. There was no shouting down of a disgruntled minority by a majority vote among his selves. It was as if there were in him a presiding chairman who, in the solemn, holy silence of inwardness, took the sense of the meeting. I would suggest that the Quaker method of conducting business meetings is also applicable to the conducting of our individual lives, inwardly.

—Thomas R. Kelly, *A Testament of Devotion,* pp. 116–118

HEAR, O Israel: The LORD our God is one LORD; and you shall love the LORD your God with all your heart, and with all your soul, and with all your might.

—Deuteronomy 6:4–5 (RSV)

GOD's nature should powerfully comfort us because He is pure unity without any non-essential multiplicity of difference even in the abstract. Everything that is in Him is God Himself.

•   •   •   •   •

Or again, a heart is said to be divided when it is dispersed over many things or towards many ends. But "every kingdom divided against itself shall be brought to desolation." Taking this even in the literal sense we observe that any virtue which is divided declines, is extinguished or decays. See the passage near the beginning of the first book of Augustine's *De Ordine,* where he says: "The soul which goes forth into multiplicity is greedily pursuing poverty, all unaware that she can only avoid it by keeping herself separate and apart." And then he adds: "The more she strives to embrace, the more she suffers want." He gives this illustration: "Just as in a circle, however large it may be, there is a single centre upon which everything converges . . . which holds sway over all by virtue, as it were, of a certain law of equality, so that if you were to go out from it in any direction, everything would be lost by the very act of advancing into multiplicity: so the soul poured forth from itself is torn asunder by a sort of universality and wasted away by real poverty or falsehood, inasmuch as it is compelled by its nature everywhere to seek the One and is prevented by multiplicity from finding it."

—Meister Eckhart, *Treatises and Sermons,* p. 219

EXERCISE 2

Acknowledge your negative selves

This week give your attention to your negative emotions and try to separate from them. We all have many negative selves—selves which lie or twist the truth, selves which complain or show off, or feel that they are not properly treated or given the attention they deserve, or selves that are irritable or disregard what others think. And then there are those selves that are filled with their own importance and are always upset when things do not go according to their plans or the schedules they have worked out. Try to be conscious of those demanding, violent, overanxious or jealous selves that give you a negative way of feeling and responding to events in life.

Whenever you feel a negative reaction in yourself or become aware of a shadow self, stand back from it and look at it and observe it. This is extremely difficult but, if you can do it, it will give you detachment. In the midst of the turmoil of your feelings, try to step into that quiet place in yourself—your own inner holy of holies. You may find of help the Scripture, "Be still, and know that I am God" (Ps. 46:10, RSV), or the single word God.

To be present to the indwelling God is to separate from negative emotions. When we stop identifying with our own negative states, they do not have the same power to control us. This does not mean that we can disclaim responsibility for any of our destitute selves. We are to take a pastoring, shepherding responsibility toward the lost and broken and ugly in our own inner world. In Scripture it is written these are the ones for whom Christ came. When you are able to acknowledge your negative selves and to separate from them, ask yourself questions concerning them. What called them into action? What are their yearnings? What fear is each based on? What is the aim of each? What speech does each make? How does each justify itself? What are the things that nourish and keep these negative selves alive?

Continue to read meditatively the selections that follow. Include in your journal your dialogue with the authors and your dialogue with your own life.

THE ONLY PERSON who is morally acceptable in the eyes of the new ethic is the person who has accepted his shadow problem—the person, that is to say, who has become conscious of his own negative side. The danger which constantly threatens the human race and which has dominated history up to the present time arises out of the "untestedness" of leaders who may actually be men of integrity as understood by the old ethic, but whose unconscious and unheeded counter-reactions have generally made more "history" than their conscious attitudes. It is precisely because we realise today that the unconscious is often, if not always, a more powerful determinant in the life of a man than his conscious attitude, his will and his intentions, that we can no longer pretend to be satisfied with a so-called "positive outlook" which is no more than a symptom of the conscious mind.

—Erich Neumann, *Depth Psychology and a New Ethic,* pp. 91–92

A NINE-YEAR-OLD boy had a violent temper that could at times sweep him into a frenzy of exultant rage; he had also a quick intuition that perceived the vulnerable spots in the other person and showed how his anger could make cruel use of them.

The world was his potential enemy. Anyone who thwarted him —his mother, his teacher, his playmate—instantly became the adversary to be overcome by violence. At these times he *was* the hate that took possession of him.

He had also another hate, "that old beast Hitler," whom his father, an army officer, was fighting. He indignantly denied suggestions that the intensity of his hatred of Hitler was related to a disturbing intuition that a Hitler who lived in him was getting stronger than he. *He* had no Hitler.

Who was it, then, who took control over him and made him try to bully other children and terrorize his mother by his prolonged storms of violence? It sounded like Hitler; it acted like Hitler.

He refused to discuss the inner Hitler, but his imagination became caught in trying to discover what made the outer Hitler "tick." At moments one could see his intuition turn inward, recognizing similarities between the two Hitlers, the inner and the outer, but his intuition was allowed freedom; no moral was driven home. One day, after talking of how Hitler enjoyed being swept into storms of anger, and working himself up into a frenzy of excitement, he was silent for some time, and then announced, "I'm not going to have that old Hitler running me any more." That day his battle with Hitler became an inner conflict, and his struggle was no longer primarily with his mother or his teacher or his playmates but with Hitler, the shadow personality within his own psyche.

He began to talk to the inner Hitler. In this way he succeeded in one of the greatest tasks of our present day—that is, *to introvert war.* "For Hitler was the most prodigious personification of all human inferiorities. . . . He represented the shadow, the inferior part of everybody's personality, in an overwhelming degree, and this is another reason why they fell for him."

Watching this inner warfare, the boy could see how the Hitler force rose within him, making him feel strong and powerful when he was really overpowered by Hitler. Seeing Hitler as a power that took possession of him, he could disidentify from him and see a self that could oppose him, a self that could choose between the forces of good and evil in the conflict within the psyche. In interiorizing his own war, he played his small (and great) part in war or peace in the world.

For every war has its beginning in the heart and mind of man. The primary battle is with the inner enemy. Until a man has conquered in himself that which causes war, he contributes, consciously or unconsciously, to warfare in the world. And since there cannot be a self-governing nation unless it is made of self-governing people, this child was preparing himself to be a citizen of a world in which peace is not a static concept but a creative act of inner conquest.

—Frances G. Wickes, *The Inner World of Choice,* pp. 33–34

MANY EFFORTS TO DIRECT, predict, or control are in reality flights from experience or forms of self-denial. In actuality man is not predictable; man is forever impermanent. Though he exists in a substantial way, he is always discovering new avenues of expression —not only because there are many ways in which he can develop his potentialities but also because there are unpredictable forces in the universe and in other men that influence his development and his experience. No matter how genuine a relationship may be, there will always be stresses and storms, to bring unexpected words, to make one impotent and afraid, to make one feel the terribleness of not being able to count on the other person, to create the despairing feeling that breaks in love can never be repaired. But one lives and loves, and suffers and forgets, and begins again—perhaps even thinking that this time, this new time, is to be permanent. But man is not permanent and man is not predictable.

—Clark E. Moustakas, *Creativity and Conformity,* pp. 20–21

IF YOU direct the undiminished power of your fervor to God's world-destiny, if you do what you must do at this moment—no matter what it may be!—with your whole strength and with kavvanah, with holy intent, you will bring about the union between God and Shekhinah, eternity and time. You need not be a scholar or a sage to accomplish this. All that is necessary is to have a soul united within itself and indivisibly directed to its divine goal. The world in which you live, just as it is and not otherwse, affords you that association with God, which will redeem you and whatever divine aspect of the world you have been entrusted with. And your own character, the very qualities which make you what you are, constitutes your special approach to God, your special potential use for Him. Do not be vexed at your delight in creatures and things! But do not let it shackle itself to creatures and things; through these, press on to God. Do not rebel against your desires, but seize them and bind them to God. You shall not stifle your surging powers, but let them work at holy work, and rest a holy rest in God. All the contradictions with which the world distresses you are only that you may discover their intrinsic significance, and all the contrary trends tormenting you within yourself, only wait to be

exorcised by your word. All innate sorrow wants only to flow into
the fervor of your joy.

    —Martin Buber, *Tales of the Hasidim: Early Masters,* p. 4

THIS discovery of the complexity of human nature was accompanied
by another—the discovery of the complexity and irrationality of
human motive, the discovery that one could love and hate simultaneously, be honest and cheap, be arrogant and humble, be any
pair of opposites that one had supposed to be mutually exclusive.
This, I believe, is not common knowledge and would be incompre-
hensible to many. It has always been known, of course, by the
dramatists and the novelists. It is, in fact, a knowledge far more
disturbing to other people than to writers, for to writers it is the
grist to their mills.

    —Alan Paton, "The Challenge of Fear"
    Saturday Review, Sept. 9, 1967

I DREAMED I had a child, and even in the dream I saw it was my
life, and it was an idiot, and I ran away. But it always crept on to
my lap again, clutched at my clothes. Until I thought, if I could
kiss it, whatever in it was my own, perhaps I could sleep. And I
bent to its broken face, and it was horrible . . . but I kissed it. I
think one must finally take one's life in one's arms, Quentin.

    —Arthur Miller, *After the Fall,* p. 22

"IT IS the greatest mistake," he [Gurdjieff] said, "to think that
man is always one and the same. A man is never the same for long.
He is continually changing. He seldom remains the same even for
half an hour. We think that if a man is called Ivan he is always
Ivan. Nothing of the kind. Now he is Ivan, in another minute he is
Peter, and a minute later he is Nicholas, Sergius, Matthew, Simon.
And all of you think he is Ivan. You know that Ivan cannot do a
certain thing. He cannot tell a lie for instance. Then you find he has
told a lie and you are surprised he could have done so. And, indeed,
Ivan cannot lie; it is Nicholas who lied. And when the opportunity

presents itself *Nicholas cannot help lying.* You will be astonished when you realize what a multitude of these Ivans and Nicholases live in one man. If you learn to observe them there is no need to go to a cinema.

". . . They all call themselves 'I.' That is, they consider themselves masters and none wants to recognize another. Each of them is caliph for an hour, does what he likes regardless of everything, and, later on, the others have to pay for it. And there is no order among them whatever. Whoever gets the upper hand is master. He whips everyone on all sides and takes heed of nothing. But the next moment another seizes the whip and beats him. And so it goes on all one's life. Imagine a country where everyone can be king for five minutes and do during these five minutes just what he likes with the whole kingdom. That is our life."

—P. D. Ouspensky, *In Search of the Miraculous,* pp. 53–54

DIVIDED, THE MAN IS DREAMING

Bathed in sweat and tumult
he slakes and kills,
eats meat
and knows blood.

His other half
lies in shadow
and longs for stillness,
a corner of the evening
where birds
rest from flight:
cool grass grows at his feet,
dark mice feed
from his hands.

—John Haines, *Winter News,*
Wesleyan University Press, 1966

THERE IS THE "I," the ego, that represents what I call *myself;* then there is the *persona,* the mask that I wear to show to the world; and there is still another part that I know, or partly know, exists but which I prefer to keep hidden because it is unacceptable to the world—this is called the *shadow,* and it is usually almost entirely forgotten—that is, it becomes unconscious to myself, although it may be quite obvious to others.

—M. Esther Harding, *The 'I' and the 'Not-I,'* p. 73

CENTRAL TO ANY CONCEPTION or practice of psychotherapy is the question, what is a person? In this chapter I have advanced what seems to be a theoretically sound and clinically supported answer to this question. The question is difficult to deal with adequately because we have unquestioningly assumed the givenness of unity in the person, have assumed that a single entity was referred to by such words as "person," "self," "I," and "me." Naturalistic observation of ourselves and others, attention to what patients in psychotherapy say and do, soon challenges this presupposition, however. It becomes impressively evident that, although there is an experienced singleness in each of us, there is also an undeniable multiplicity. Thus we are confronted with the paradox of concurrent unity and plurality in the person.

As we study these phenomena, it becomes evident that one source of the apparent diversity is the person's inauthenticity, his flight from anxiety, responsibility, and guilt. By *Self*-fragmentation the patient seeks to resist that which he has come to feel cannot be borne.

Yet the resistance does not fully account for the multiple *Selves* we encounter in all people. Accordingly, I have inquired further into the nature of the *Self*-experience and have concluded that the very processes by which we learn to live in the world give rise to multiple *Selves*. Clinical evidence is mounting that for most of us the phenomenological reality is not a single *Self* but several *Selves*.

—J. F. T. Bugental, *The Search for Authenticity,* p. 216

THAT FINITE CREATURE which man places in the stead of the creator
becomes an organizing center for a separate, rebellious, runaway,
and isolated portion of his personhood. Soon this portion rises up
and rules the whole personality. Or, the victory may be incomplete;
and this portion simply makes periodic, predatory raids on the total
personality. This is what Plato defined as sin, namely, the rising
up of a part of the soul against the whole. This is what Paul Tillich
describes as "the absolutizing of the finite." That which one has
substituted for God "possesses" the total person, and exerts "de-
monic" power over self. Leslie D. Weatherhead has pointed out
that Jesus makes no reference to devils (though the conversations
around him were full of reference to them) apart from the context
of disease and the possible exception of the storm on the lake.
Nevertheless, Jesus did insist repeatedly that no man could serve
two masters; and purity of heart, the priority of the vision of God,
oneness of devotion were all related to the maintenance of the integrity of the total person. Likewise later persons, captured by the
singleness of heart of obedience to Christ, could say that a double-
minded man is unstable in all his ways.
—Wayne E. Oates, *Religious Dimensions of Personality,* p. 200

WORRY IS A FORM of identifying. Literally, the word has the meaning of tearing and twisting, or choking and strangling; it was
originally connected with the word "wring," which is still used
in the expression "wringing one's hands," one of the outward
signs of worry. You will remember that every psychological or
inner state finds some outer representation via the moving centre—
that is, it is represented in some particular muscular movements or
contractions, etc. You may have noticed that a state of worry is
often reflected by a contracted wrinkling of the forehead or a
twisting of the hands. States of joy never have this representation.
Negative states, states of worry, or fear, or anxiety, or depression,
represent themselves in the muscles by contraction, flexion, being
bowed down, etc. (and often, also, by weakness in the muscles),

whereas opposite emotional states are reflected into the moving centre as expansion, as standing upright, as extension of the limbs, relaxing of tension, and usually by a feeling of strength. *To stop worry,* people who worry and thereby frown too much or pucker up and corrugate their foreheads, clench their fists, almost cease breathing, etc., should begin here—by *relaxing the muscles* expressing the emotional state, and freeing the breath. Relaxing in general has behind it, esoterically speaking, the idea of *preventing* negative states. Negative states are less able to come when a person is in a state of relaxation. That is why it is said so often that it is necessary to practise relaxing every day, by passing the attention over the body and deliberately relaxing all tense muscles.

．　　．　　．　　．　　．

Now the level of your being enters into request as much or more than your knowledge. You may *ask* intellectually for happiness but not see how factors that govern your being, as love of your negative states, your grievances, your secret jealousies, your laziness, your dislikes, and so on, are asking for something quite different, and that the Universe is responding to these factors in your being that you are secretly willing and affirming without seeing that you are. Understand that *full request* must contain both thought and will—formulation and emotional desire. The side of knowledge is the side of thought and a man can only think from his knowledge. The side of being wills, and a man only *wills* what he desires. If you love negative states, then your will is of this quality. Your love is your will; it will attract the response belonging to it. Only self-knowledge will make you aware of your state of being and this begins with self-observation. Enough has been said here on this subject—namely, that a person may be getting *responses* he does not expect or desire, without seeing that he is attracting them because he is making *requests* for them that he is not aware of.

—Maurice Nicoll, *Psychological Commentaries,*
Vol. 1, pp. 136, 154

"AGAIN I tell you this: if two of you agree on earth about any request you have to make, that request will be granted by my heavenly Father. For where two or three have met together in my name, I am there among them."

—Matt. 18:19–20 (NEB)

IF MAN were a unity instead of being a multiplicity, he would have true individuality. He would be one and so would have one will. The illusion, therefore, that a man has about himself that he is one refers to a possibility. Man *can* attain unity of being. He can reach his true individuality. But it is precisely this illusion that stands first of all in the way of man's attainment of this possibility. For as long as a man imagines he has something, he will not seek for it. Why should a man strive for something that he has never doubted for a moment that he possesses already? This is one of the effects of the imagination, which fills up, as it were, what is lacking or makes it appear that we are like this, or like that, when actually we are the reverse.

—Maurice Nicoll, *Psychological Commentaries,* Vol. 1, p. 23

WE WANT TO GROW undeformed: to dare to know ourself and be ourself. We want to identify ourself more and more with the great inner "I" at the centre, and less and less with the small outer "Me," who is whirling around on the rim of the wheel of time. Our need is to be re-born, not once nor twice but constantly, continually, that we may digest the whole of our earth experience and so be ready to inherit eternal life. To move from blindness to sight, from shutness to openness, from bondage to freedom—that is our journey and our destiny.

—E. Graham Howe and L. Le Mesurier, *The Open Way,* p. 136

JESUS ASKED HIM, "What is your name?"
    "Legion," he replied.

—Luke 8:30 (NEB)

HOLY FATHER, protect by the power of thy name those whom thou hast given me, that they may be one, as we are one.

—John 17:11 (NEB)

IN HIM the whole building is bonded together and grows into a holy temple in the Lord. In him you too are being built with all the rest into a spiritual dwelling for God.

—Ephesians 2:21–22 (NEB)

PART TWO

FROM JUDGMENT
TO EMPATHY

Every day there deepens in me an understanding of the Church as a laboratory of change. This is what Christianity is about. The New Testament is talking about a radical kind of change: "Once you were no people but now you are God's people";[1] once you were dead, now you are alive; once you were lost, now you are found. The writers strain for language to describe a change so dramatic that all words fall short: "new being," "new creation," "new birth," "new covenant." When they turn to poetry they say it is like being "born again."

If the early Church had had the vocabulary of modern psychology its task would have been easier, for it was talking about a new kind of consciousness. It wanted its people to have a "coming into existence" experience, which is the term that Raymond Rogers uses. The people of the Way were a people growing in consciousness. This is what it meant to belong to the Church. It

1. 1 Peter 2:10 (RSV).

was a Church concerned with the awakening of men to that whole world in themselves that they were not aware of. The cry was, "Awake, O sleeper, and arise from the dead, and Christ shall give you light."[2] And who was this Christ? He was the One who knew what was in all men and was calling them to be who they might be. In every conversation He was helping someone to be in on more of his life. To the impetuous, unstable Peter, he said, "Now I tell you that you are Peter the rock. . . ." It was Jung who read some of the scathing words of Revelation and commented that it was not for nothing that the Apostle John was nicknamed "Son of Thunder" by Christ. The call today is the same: for men to awaken to the hidden depths in themselves. Grace is that moment when we see in ourselves what we had not seen before.

What has growing in *consciousness* to do with the change the New Testament is talking about, and the chief end of man which is to glorify God and enjoy him forever? Everything. Modern psychology has given us the image of the iceberg—most of it submerged and out of sight—to illustrate the relationship of the conscious to the unconscious. Not only does the jagged tip showing above the waters represent all that we know of ourselves, but it also follows that it is the only part of us with which we can praise God, and listen to Him and serve Him. More than that, modern man with the cry "Who am I?" is discovering that this self that he sees and thinks he knows so well may be a self that is bolstered by illusions and self-deceit, having very little connection with his real self. It may, indeed, be the life that he is asked to lose in order to find his life. It is against the backdrop of that picture of the iceberg that this age is given the command, "Love the Lord thy God with all thy heart and soul and mind."

What can the man of faith do with that command today? He has heard too much to stay with traditional understandings of the Christian pilgrimage. He cannot plead ignorance of the "divided self," or of the unconscious. There is no way for him to take seriously the command of his Lord except by being on the journey

2. Eph. 5:14 (RSV).

of coming into possession of himself. This is the change that the writers of Scripture spoke about and the early Church proclaimed with all the understanding and language available to them.

The exercises and meditative readings in this book are to help us to be on the journey of becoming more conscious, or more whole, or more holy. It is change that we must struggle for, but when it comes it is always by the grace of God. It is His Spirit that broods over the void and darkness of our lives, and over the face of the abyss in us. It is God who says, "Let there be light." It is God who sends a Son that by the power of the Resurrection what is unknown in us may be lifted up and made known.

It is the amazing love of God that wills a man grow straight and tall in his soul. This is why in the cataloguing of sins some are called deadly. Not, as we have thought, for moralistic reasons, but because they block growth in us, and in others. God's judgment turns out to be His love, for it calls us back to the creating of our own lives. Most of the sins on that famous list of seven have us looking for the meaning of our lives somewhere "out there." Take envy, or lust, or greed—they have their basis in the feeling that another has what we need, or can give us what we need, or that somehow out there in life we can acquire what we must have, when what is essential for authentic life lies within our own being. It is the work of the Holy Spirit to call it forth, and our awakening to this is our awakening to life in Jesus Christ. "When the Spirit of truth comes, he will guide you into all the truth."[3] And we answer, "Come, Lord Jesus!"[4]

The ministry of our Lord was a ministry of awakening sleeping humanity to a world within and a world beyond. In the *Codex Bezae* is a saying of Jesus that Erich Neumann, agreeing with Carl Jung, suggests might well be the motto for a new morality: "Man, if thou knowest what thou doest, thou art blessed, but if thou knowest not, thou art accursed, and a transgressor of the law."[5] It is reflected

3. John 16:13 (RSV).   4. Rev. 22:20 (RSV).
5. Erich Neumann, *Depth Psychology and a New Ethic* (New York: G. P. Putnam's Sons, 1969), p. 143.

in one of the final prayers of Jesus, "Father, forgive them; for they
know not what they do."[6]

The exercises in this unit are concerned with the movement from
judgment to empathy because being critical is another way of
failing to deal with our own lives. Not only does it keep us from
being conscious of what blocks our own growth, but it prevents
our exercising those gifts of knowing and caring which are smoth-
ered by critical and negative selves. I have chosen this subject above
others to include here because it is one that I have struggled with
in my own life. As I worked with it, I observed how critical attitudes are destroyers of community while their opposites—empathy
and understanding—support and nurture lives.

Another early observation was how little being critical of someone takes care of the feelings out of which criticism flows. Critical
words seem to give relief to critical feelings, but if you will continue to be aware of your feelings after your words are ended, you
will note that they did not, after all, cancel out your grievance.
Your complaint is still locked in you, demanding another kind of
attention.

This does not mean that there is not a time and place to examine
and judge and express criticism. It is not, however, the valid role
of critic or the development of legitimate critical faculties that we
want to consider in these weeks. Rather we are asked to observe
in ourselves a censorious kind of criticism that cuts us off from
others and keeps us from exercising responsibility for our own lives.
Each of us is to become an authority on the subject of his own
critical selves.

It is suggested that the Scriptural meditation for the four weeks
spent on this unit be Matthew 7:1–5 (RSV), in which Jesus talks
very plainly about the shadow self and the moral imperative that
rests on each individual to struggle for consciousness.

Judge not, that you be not judged. For with the judgment you pronounce you will be judged, and the measure you give will be the measure

6. Luke 23:34 (RSV).

you get. Why do you see the speck that is in your brother's eye, but do not notice the log that is in your own eye? Or how can you say to your brother, "Let me take the speck out of your eye," when there is the log in your own eye? You hypocrite, first take the log out of your own eye, and then you will see clearly to take the speck out of your brother's eye.

Meditate on this Scripture each day, carry it about with you, and discover in your daily encounters its practical application for your life. Four weeks is a long time to cleave to a portion of Scripture, but try it. This much time may be needed to show us anything about ourselves. If it is to change our natural bias or way of responding, it will have to strike its roots down deep in us. How many ever give Scripture this opportunity? We go from one good insight to another, sometimes exuberant over our findings. This is different from giving words and the Word an opportunity to move and work in us and disrupt usual thought patterns. Goethe says that we listen more to our own words than to our neighbors' and take from our neighbors' what pleases us. Then he adds:

> Nearly the same is the case with books; for every one will
> Find himself in the book, unless in his strength he decides on
> Putting himself into it and amalgamating the substance.[7]

We know this to be true, for the books we read change us so little even when we applaud them. This, then, is in the nature of an experiment, to see if we can put ourselves enough into Scripture for it to yield its secret and for the substance of it to be amalgamated with the cells and fibers of our beings.

Keep your journal.

7. "First Epistle."

EXERCISE 3

Observe times when you are critical

Try to be aware of those situations in which you are being critical of another either in your conversation or inwardly in your spirit. How does this affect your attitude toward the other? Listen to the inner conversation of that self that criticizes. Become familiar with how it explains and justifies itself. Do not try to change it. Just observe it so that you can become familiar with its comings and goings.

Perhaps your criticism is directed primarily toward a group. It may be your small church group, or even the larger congregation, or your business associates. This needs to be examined in the same way.

THE IDEAL OF "unprejudiced objectivity" occupies a middle position between two opposites which are expressed as "passing judgment" on the one hand, and "agreeing offhand" on the other. To be in touch with another person, therefore, is to recognize his difference from oneself, and, at the same time, to respect this difference. To pass judgment is to imply that the other person should alter himself; to agree offhand is to imply that one's own attitude is less valid than that of the other person. The ideal is a relationship in which each respects the other as a person in his own right, without trying to alter the other.

.   .   .   .   .

To incorporate another person is to swallow him up, to overwhelm him, and to destroy him; and thus to treat him ultimately as less than a whole person. To identify with another person is to lose oneself, to submerge one's own identity in that of the other, to be overwhelmed, and hence to treat oneself ultimately as less than a whole person. To pass judgment, in Jung's sense, is to place oneself in an attitude of superiority; to agree offhandedly is to place oneself in an attitude of inferiority . . . the personality can cease to exist in two ways—either by destroying the other, or being absorbed by the other—and maturity in interpersonal relationships demands that neither oneself nor the other shall disappear, but that each shall contribute to the affirmation and realization of the other's personality.

—Anthony Storr, *The Integrity of Personality,* pp. 41–42, 43

ONE PROBLEM that I face in relationship with another person is that I assume certain things about that individual and expect him to live up to my assumptions. The problem is one of projecting my personal expectations upon another, thereby making him responsible for that which is in me. In growing into maturity there needs to come the time when I can separate that which is my problem from that of the other person, arriving at a position which enables the other person to be himself without carrying the responsibility of being what I expect him to be at the same time. Actually we can never get to the core of the relationship until the assumptions of each individual are seen for what they are.

In other words, we can call this the conflict between idealism and realism. Idealism in this sense is not based on the potential of what might be, but a perverted idealism which demands that another be what I want and need him to be. I prefer to use the terminology, assumption-definition, rather than idealism-realism. Most of our assumptions about other people or structures usually do not take into consideration the total picture; therefore they tend to be only partial pictures with little genuine validity.

—Bill Shiflett, "Community, Commitment and
Judgment in Mission" (unpublished paper)

GOD HATES visionary dreaming; it makes the dreamer proud and pretentious. The man who fashions a visionary ideal of community demands that it be realized by God, by others, and by himself. He enters the community of Christians with his demands, sets up his own laws, and judges the brethren and God Himself accordingly. He stands adamant, a living reproach to all others in the circle of brethren. He acts as if he is the creator of the Christian community, as if his dream binds men together. When things do not go his way, he calls the effort a failure. When his ideal picture is destroyed, he sees the community going to smash. So he becomes, first an accuser of his brethren, then an accuser of God, and finally the despairing accuser of himself.

—Dietrich Bonhoeffer, *Life Together*, pp. 27–28

HE WAS IMPOSSIBLE. It wasn't that he didn't attend to his work: on the contrary, he took endless pains over the tasks he was given. But his manner of behavior brought him into conflict with everybody and, in the end, began to have an adverse effect on everything he had to do with.

When the crisis came and the whole truth had to come out, he laid the blame on us: in his conduct there was nothing, absolutely nothing to reproach. His self-esteem was so strongly bound up, apparently, with the idea of his innocence, that one felt a brute as one demonstrated, step by step, the contradictions in his defense and, bit by bit, stripped him naked before his own eyes. But justice to others demanded it.

When the last rag of a lie had been taken from him and we felt there was nothing more to be said, out it came with stifled sobs.

"But why did you never help me, why didn't you tell me what to do? You knew that I always felt you were against me. And fear and insecurity drove me further and further along the course you now condemn me for having taken. It's been so hard—everything. One day, I remember, I was so happy: one of you said that something I had produced was quite good—"

So, in the end, we were, in fact, to blame. We had not voiced our criticisms, but we had allowed them to stop us from giving him a single word of acknowledgment, and in this way had barred every road to improvement.

For it is always the stronger one who is to blame. We lack life's patience. Instinctively, we try to eliminate a person from our sphere of responsibility as soon as the outcome of this particular experiment by Life appears, in our eyes, to be a failure. But Life pursues her experiments far beyond the limitations of our judgment. This is also the reason why, at times, it seems so much more difficult to live than to die.

—Dag Hammarskjöld, *Markings,* pp. 31–32

WE MUST not be conceited, challenging one another to rivalry, jealous of one another. If a man should do something wrong, my brothers, on a sudden impulse, you who are endowed with the Spirit must set him right again very gently. Look to yourself, each one of you: you may be tempted too. Help one another to carry these heavy loads, and in this way you will fulfill the law of Christ.

For if a man imagines himself to be somebody, when he is nothing, he is deluding himself. Each man should examine his own conduct for himself; then he can measure his achievement by comparing himself with himself and not with anyone else. For everyone has his own proper burden to bear.

—Galatians 5:26, 6:1–5 (NEB)

WE CERTAINLY cannot "know ourselves" if we refuse to recognize the evil that is in us, and the same thing is true about those we love. It is even more difficult to accept their ignorances and faults than it is to accept our own. There seems a kind of disloyalty in any, even silent criticism. But there is confusion here. The greatest love loves in spite of, and not because of, the qualities of the beloved. Why should they be perfect when we are so imperfect? Has the motive of personal advantage crept unawares into what seemed all unselfish desire for them? Certainly life would be easier for us if we could always admire and approve them, feeling confidence in their rightness. It would reassure us if they responded to our ideals of them and for them. But only unresolved conflict or the dangers of phantasy come from unreality. To assume that what we wish is ours already, or can be swiftly brought about by an effort of our will, or by an appeal to the Divine Will, is a refusal of reality.

There are two troubles here. First the irrational feeling that whatever degree of enlightenment we may have gained ourselves ought simultaneously to have been gained by our families and friends. Why cannot our experiences be pooled and passed on? But they are individual experiences, not mass productions; neither simultaneous nor identical, but separated by years, or perhaps by lives. This is painful but must be accepted. If we all knew and understood and accepted at the same time, that would be heaven. This is earth.

—E. Graham Howe and L. Le Mesurier, *The Open Way,*
pp. 126–127

CHRISTIANITY does not recognize the fixed types of "the wicked" and of "the righteous." An evil-doer may turn into a righteous man, and *vice versa.* St. John of the Ladder says: "You will be careful not to condemn sinners if you remember that Judas was one of the Apostles and the thief was one of a band of murderers; but in one moment the miracle of regeneration took place in him." This is why Christ teaches us "judge not, that ye be not judged." Up to the hour of death no one knows what may happen to a man and what a complete change he may undergo nor does anyone know what happens to him at the hour of death, on a plane inaccessible to us. This is why Christianity regards "the wicked" differently than this world does; it does not allow a sharp division of mankind into two halves, the good and the wicked—a division by which moral theories set much store.

Christianity alone teaches that the past can be wiped out; it knows the mystery of forgetting and canceling the past. . . .

—Nicolas Berdyaev, *The Destiny of Man*, p. 108

WHY DO YOU pass judgment on your brother? Or you, why do you despise your brother? For we shall all stand before the judgment seat of God; for it is written,

"As I live, says the Lord, every knee shall bow to me,
and every tongue shall give praise to God."

So each of us shall give account of himself to God.

Then let us no more pass judgment on one another, but rather decide never to put a stumbling-block or hindrance in the way of a brother.

—Romans 14:10–13 (RSV)

THE GROWING TREE

Rabbi Uri taught:

"Man is like a tree. If you stand in front of a tree and watch it incessantly to see how it grows and to see how much it has grown, you will see nothing at all. But tend to it at all times, prune the runners, and keep the vermin from it, and—all in good time—it

will come into its growth. It is the same with man: all that is necessary is for him to overcome his obstacles, and he will thrive and
grow. But it is not right to examine him every hour to see how
much has been added to his growth."

—Martin Buber, *Tales of the Hasidim: Later Masters*, p. 148

EXERCISE 4

Find in yourself what you criticize in another

What you criticize in another, try to find in yourself. We want to discover our dark selves, not in order that they may be condemned and banished out of sight, but in order that we may have conversation with them and they may lead us to the light. This is the promise if we will attend to them.

An added discipline for this week might be to say nothing negative about anyone else or about yourself. This will give you more energy for inner work on the subject. If you find it a difficult discipline to keep, do not be discouraged. A discipline is to help us learn, and there is often more learning in failure than in success.

Continue to use the selections following each exercise for meditative reading.

My son, in all modesty, keep your self-respect
and value yourself at your true worth.
Who will speak up for a man who is his own enemy,
or respect one who disparages himself?
                        —Ecclesiasticus 10:28–29 (NEB)

THE "OTHER" in us always seems to us alien and unacceptable; but if we allow ourselves to be aggrieved and hurt by it, then it goes into us, and we are the richer for a piece of self-knowledge.

—C. G. Jung, *Civilization in Transition,* Vol. 10 in Collected Works, p. 486, par. 918

ONLY A FOOL is interested in other people's guilt, since he cannot alter it. The wise man learns only from his own guilt. He will ask himself: Who am I that all this should happen to me? To find the answer to this fateful question he will look into his own heart.

—C. G. Jung, *Psychology and Alchemy,* Vol. 10 in Collected Works, p. 112, par. 152

BUT WE CANNOT change anyone else; we can change only ourselves, and then usually only when the elements that are in need of reform have become conscious through their reflection in someone else.

—M. Esther Harding, *The 'I' and the 'Not-I,'* p. 75

THE centre of all iniquity is invariably found to lie a few miles behind the enemy lines. Because the individual has this same primitive psychology, every attempt to bring these age-old projections to consciousness is felt as irritating. Naturally one would like to have better relations with one's fellows, but only on the condition that *they* live up to *our* expectations—in other words, that they become willing carriers of our projections.

—C. G. Jung, *The Structure and Dynamics of the Psyche,* Vol. 8 in Collected Works, pp. 271–272, par. 517

THIS WAR has pitilessly revealed to civilized man that he is still a barbarian, and has at the same time shown what an iron scourge lies in store for him if ever again he should be tempted to make his neighbour responsible for his own evil qualities. The psychology of the individual is reflected in the psychology of the nation. What the nation does is done also by each individual, and so long as the individual continues to do it, the nation will do likewise. Only a change in the attitude of the individual can initiate a change in the psychology of the nation.

—C. G. Jung, *Two Essays on Analytical Psychology,* Vol. 7
in Collected Works, p. 4

WE CANNOT stand the sight of our dark side, so we repress it, push it under, thinking we have thereby disposed of it. But we have not. We have simply pushed it into a place where it both has us in its grip and automatically projects itself on the person or the nation we do not like; so the tension we will not stand in ourselves is carelessly and irresponsibly cast out to increase the tension and strife and anguish of our world. As we have mentioned, Jung saw it as a psychological law that what we will not suffer inwardly through conscious recognition of our shadow, we will suffer outwardly as the result of our unconscious projections into the world around us. He thereby gives Christians the most awesome charge that they can possibly receive throughout their lives: the withdrawal of their projections upon others, and dealing with their shadow themselves. Here one almost senses the dimension of the "hellfire and brimstone" preaching, once so characteristic of the church's message. Has it faded out of church evangelism only to rise anew in the awesome heights and depths of the new psychology?

—Charles B. Hanna, *The Face of the Deep,* pp. 100–101

SELF-RECRIMINATIONS as a rule are complicated in structure. There is not any one single answer as to their meaning, and those who insist on getting simple answers to psychological questions will necessarily go astray. To begin with, self-recriminations are an unavoidable consequence of the categorical character of the need to appear perfect. Two simple analogies from everyday life may illustrate: If for any reason it is important for a person to win a game of ping-pong, he will be angry at himself for making an awkward play; if for any reason it is important for him to make a good impression at an interview he will be angry at himself for having forgotten to mention a point which would have put him in a good light, and may scold himself afterwards and say how silly it was of him not to have talked about that point.

．　．　．　．　．

Perfectionistic persons, as has been said, are deeply afraid of anyone recognizing that their façade is only a façade; hence their madding fear of criticism and reproaches. In this regard their self-recriminations are an attempt to anticipate reproaches and, by raising them themselves, to prevent others from making them—even more, to appease others by demonstrating their apparent severity toward themselves and to elicit reassurance.

．　．　．　．　．

The practice of shifting reproaches from others to oneself is often based on the philosophy that someone has to be blamed whenever anything adverse happens. Usually, if not always, persons who build up a colossal apparatus to maintain the semblance of perfection are highly apprehensive of impending disaster. They feel as if they were living under a suspended sword which may fall down at any moment, although they may not be aware of these fears. They have a fundamental incapacity to face life's ups and downs in a matter-of-fact way. They cannot reconcile themselves to the fact that life is not calculable like a mathematical task, that it is to some extent like an adventure or like a gamble, subject to good and ill luck, full of unpredictable difficulties and risks, unforeseen and unforeseeable perplexities. As a means of reassurance they cling to the belief that life is calculable and controllable. Hence they believe it is the fault of someone if something goes wrong, for this makes it possible to avoid the unpleasant and frightening realization that life is incalculable and uncontrollable. If such persons are for

any reason stopped from reproaching others they will take on themselves the blame for adverse happenings.

—Karen Horney, M.D., *New Ways in Psychoanalysis,* pp. 239,
240, 243

THERE IS A TOMBSTONE near my childhood home in England which
admonishes the passer-by: "The faults ye see in others take care to
shun. If you'll only look at home there's enough to be done."

—M. Esther Harding, *The 'I' and the 'Not-I,'* p. 57

HE WHO DESIRES to become aware of the hidden light must lift the
feeling of fear up to its source. And he can accomplish this if he
judges himself and all he does. For then he sheds all fears and lifts
fear that has fallen down. But if he does not judge himself, he will
be judged from on high, and this judgment will come upon him in
the guise of countless things, and all the things in the world will
become messengers of God who carry out the judgment on this man.

—Martin Buber, *Ten Rungs: Hasidic Sayings,* p. 73

THIS GUILT-FEELING based on the existence of the shadow is dis-
charged from the system in the same way by both the individual and
the collective—that is to say, by the phenomenon of the *projection
of the shadow.* The shadow, which is in conflict with the acknowledged values, cannot be accepted as a negative part of one's own
psyche and is therefore projected—that is, it is transferred to the
outside world and experienced as an outside object. It is combated,
punished, and exterminated as "the alien out there" instead of being
dealt with as "one's own inner problem."

The way in which the old ethic provides for the elimination of
these feelings of guilt and the discharge of the excluded negative
forces is in fact one of the gravest perils confronting mankind.
What we have in mind here is that classic psychological expedient—
the institution of a scapegoat. This technique for attempting a solution of the problem is to be found wherever human society exists.
It is, however, best known as a ritual of Judaism. Here the purifica-

tion of the collective was carried out by solemnly heaping all impurity and evil upon the head of the scapegoat, which was then sent away into exile in the wilderness—to Azazel.

The unconscious psychic conflicts of groups and masses find their most spectacular outlets in epidemic eruptions such as wars and revolutions, in which the unconscious forces which have accumulated in the collective get the upper hand and "make history." The *scapegoat psychology* is in fact an example of an early, though still inadequate, attempt to deal with these unconscious conflicts. This psychology shapes the inner life of nations just as much as it does their international relationships. . . .

—Erich Neumann, *Depth Psychology and a New Ethic*,
p. 50

ANY SUDDEN CHANGE in a person's position in society is liable to arouse anxieties concerning his identity. As a consequence he may then begin to project his own weaknesses and vices on to members of feared outgroups. There are many ways in which the psyche of such persons may deal with evidence and argument incompatible with the picture of reality built up and sustained by their fears. The simplest way is to avoid people likely to present a case that will disturb, and similarly to avoid their meetings and publications. Where this stratagem fails, and reality has to be met, simple logical fallacies in reasoning offer a wide range of opportunities for avoiding painful conclusions. Language too is rich in opportunities for masking and mistranslating reality according to inner psychic needs. It would not be difficult to compile a thesaurus of contrasting terms in common use: the one set to describe qualities of people belonging to one's own group, the other set to describe the same attributes when possessed by members of the group that is feared or hated: e.g.,

> thrifty, stingy;
> generous, spendthrift;
> eager, grasping;
> determined, fanatical;

brave, foolhardy;
leisurely, idle;
smart, flashy;
statesman, political maneuverer.
—R. V. Sampson, *The Psychology of Power,* pp. 204–205

NO ONE can develop alone. Now relationship is possible only through the contact of inner worlds. We meet through our inner worlds. To understand another you must enter into his inner world, but this is not possible if you have not entered your own inner world. The first step therefore towards entering consciously into and understanding the position of another is attained through entering into and understanding the position of *oneself* and unless this step is taken, to as full a degree as is possible, there is little or no possibility of entering into and understanding the position of another person. The entry into oneself begins with self-observation and the understanding of oneself comes through long self-study. . . . For this reason, merely to think that one is capable of entering into and understanding the position of another person, and even giving help, *as one is*—and this illusion is very common—is to misunderstand entirely the nature of human contact and the universal difficulties that attend this impulse, which so frequently ends in disaster or some sort of compromise which, as often as not, is the breeding-ground of bitterness, mutual criticism, hostility and even worse emotional states and trains of thought. No one as he is mechanically—that is, as formed by life and its influences—can enter into and understand another, and, from that, give help, unless he already knows from his own self-observation, self-study and insight and work on himself, what is in the other person. Only through self-knowledge is knowledge of others practically possible. Only by seeing, knowing and understanding what is in yourself can you see, know and understand what is in another person. One of the greatest evils of human relationship is that people make no attempt to enter into one another's position but merely criticize one another without any restraint and do not possess any inner check to this mechanical criticism owing to the absence of any insight into themselves and their own glaring crudities, faults and shortcomings. As a result, not only do they not help each other, but the normal balance of things is upset, and by this I mean that an accumulation of wrong or evil psychic material is formed daily in human relationships and, in fact, in everyone's life, which should never exist if people saw themselves and others simultaneously, and in this way could neutralize the effects of their conduct day by day. This lack of psychological responsibility, both to oneself and to others, is perhaps especially characteristic of modern times and is the source of one part of the widespread modern unhappiness that marks the present age, in which, amongst other things, there is a decline in even ordinary human kindness, with a resulting hardness which is among the most dangerous factors in regard to the future, and which effectually stops all possibility of the right development of the emotional life.

—Maurice Nicoll, *Psychological Commentaries,* Vol. 1,
pp. 149–150

EXERCISE 5

Observe your own reactions to criticism

Observe how you react to criticism—criticism of yourself, of your friends, of your group or groups. Do you ever ask for an opinion of how you are doing your work and of how you might do it better? Do you listen when you are criticized? Do you grow angry? Are you defensive? Do you try to justify yourself? Many of us will find that one word of criticism cancels out ten of praise. We hear criticism as representative of the person's total response to our total person—rather than as a comment on one aspect of our multifaceted self. This exercise is concerned with helping us to become aware of our own individual response to criticism.

If you dare risk it, ask someone for a critical evaluation of something which is important to you, but do not do this carelessly or without inner preparation. It may be more painful than you would guess.

UNLESS AN INDIVIDUAL'S sense of identity and purpose are securely located in a metaphysic which transcends the claims of particularist groups, he will be very prone to derive his sense of significance from the values of the group or groups with which he identifies himself. Accordingly any threat to those groups will be experienced as a threat to the stability of the individual ego identifying with them. . . .

—R. V. Sampson, *The Psychology of Power,* p. 203

ANIMALS ARE such agreeable friends—they ask no questions, they pass no criticisms.

George Eliot, *Mr. Gilfil's Love-Story* (*Oxford Dictionary of Quotations,* p. 196)

PEOPLE ASK YOU for criticism, but they only want praise.

—W. Somerset Maugham, *Of Human Bondage* (*Oxford Dictionary of Quotations,* p. 335)

I DO NOT RESENT criticism, even when, for the sake of emphasis, it parts for the time with reality.

—Winston Churchill, from a speech in the House of Commons, January 22, 1941, (*Oxford Dictionary of Quotations,* p. 144)

AND SO, TOO, when someone is uncertain of himself, always needing the approval and support of others and being unduly depressed by their criticism, it means that he has no valid criterion of value from within himself. If he is disapproved of, he feels crushed; if he is not noticed, he ceases to exist; and if he is praised, he is in the seventh heaven of elation. He has little sense of his personal value, though he may give the appearance of being exceedingly egotistic, since he is always "fishing" for praise. He purrs and preens himself when it is given, literally basking in an atmosphere of approval, while he usually goes away by himself to hide his hurt if the desired notice is not forthcoming. His center of gravity is not in himself, but outside in other people. Now, of course, I do not mean to say that we ought not to take account of the judgment of our peers, but I do mean that if we do not have a valid judgment of our own actions, we should inquire whether we are not lacking in a true self, not able to differentiate between what is "I" and what "Not-I."

.   .   .   .   .

Things that belong to *me,* that are *mine,* share something of myself; they are bigger, better, more important than similar possessions of other people, and indeed they may even seem sacred, taboo. . . . Certain possessions—particular books, a particular chair—must not be usurped by another. They are sacrosanct, that is, they are extensions of myself. My pen, my pipe, my car, my sword, my family are not like other people's; they are special with a specialness that is violated only at the risk either of arousing my ire or of causing me the most acute distress, as though something in myself had been attacked.

—M. Esther Harding, *The 'I' and the 'Not-I,'* pp. 46, 71

FOR INSTANCE, some member wants to lead. Let us assume that in reality he has a good idea and wishes to engineer it into effectiveness. So far, it is a legitimate conscious matter. But it is an easy step for him to become identified with his idea, so that he becomes a blind, one-sided psychological force and no longer an individual. Instead of offering the idea for what it is worth and being willing to convince, persuade, and wait, even to relinquish it if definitely outvoted, he tries to drive or wrangle it through, unaware that he is thereby forcing his way of looking at things upon other people and approximating the typical dictator archetype.

—Eleanor Bertine, *Jung's Contribution to Our Time,* p. 117

MOST OF US associate being criticized with being punished or told we're unwanted, and often it bears this implication, especially when parents criticize their children. Only by forcing ourselves to listen to criticism can we teach ourselves that it is sometimes well intended,

and that we won't fall to pieces no matter what other people say
about us.
                    —George Weinberg, *The Action Approach*, p. 219

AS SOON as you think you are good at something and your pride and
vanity enter this idea that you are good at something, you will
always find that you are most sensitive here and most liable to become violent. In other words, you are being *something*. If you could
see all the mistakes and blunders that you make yourself, if you
could see your contradictions, if you could become conscious of your
failures, in regard to what you think you are good at, you would no
longer be sensitive or violent but tolerant and at the same time
would have more understanding. Sometimes people cannot allow
that they are not good at things because of a certain inner weakness
in them. What is this inner weakness due to? It is due to this unacknowledged side, the dark side, which, as it were, contains,
amongst other things, all that they are not willing to accept. You
may be good at a thing, but you must also acknowledge gradually,
especially as you get older and need a wider consciousness, that you
are not good at it at the same time and realize, in short, that you
are not what you thought. Then you no longer identify in the way
you did and you become simpler inside. This letting in of the other
side, of the dark or not observed side, does not weaken you, but
really strengthens you. Someone asked: "Is it bad, the dark side?"
You must understand that everything you do not acknowledge
appears at first sight bad. It is the devil because the devil is always
what is unknown, unacknowledged or not understood.
                    —Maurice Nicoll, *Psychological Commentaries*, Vol. 3,
                                                                p. 835

I WISH WE FIVE, who now love each other in Christ, could make an
agreement together. Just as others in recent times have been meeting
secretly to contrive evil deeds and heresies against His Majesty, so
we might try to meet sometimes to undeceive one another and to
advise one another as to ways in which we might amend our lives

and be more pleasing to God; for there is no one who knows himself as well as he is known by those who see him if they observe him lovingly and are anxious to help him. I say "secretly," because it is no longer the fashion to talk in this way: even preachers nowadays phrase their sermons so as not to give offense. No doubt their intention is good, and the work they do is good too, but they lead few people to amend their lives.

—St. Teresa, *Collected Works,* Vol. VIII, *Life,* p. 99

EXERCISE 6

Practice empathy

Choose a person you feel critical of and for a week try living in his world. Even though you can never know the mystery of another life, it is possible to see another more accurately and with greater understanding.

Say something of genuine praise to someone each day.

Remember that the writings are not intended to aid you in condemning yourself. Scripture tells us to love others, forgive, and not judge, but the writers knew that this is not something we can decide to do and then do. The Scriptures point us the way we are to go. They give us the task of working with our lives, for it is in that work that the Spirit comes and we learn what freedom, redemption, and the new birth are all about.

PUT OFF YOUR SHOES from your feet, for the place on which you are standing is holy ground."

—Exodus 3:5 (RSV)

WHEN A TROUT rising to a fly gets hooked on a line and finds himself unable to swim about freely, he begins with a fight which results in struggles and splashes and sometimes an escape. Often, of course, the situation is too tough for him.

In the same way the human being struggles with his environment and with the hooks that catch him. Sometimes he masters his difficulties; sometimes they are too much for him. His struggles are all that the world sees and it naturally misunderstands them. It is hard for a free fish to understand what is happening to a hooked one.

—Karl Menninger, M.D., *The Human Mind*, p. 3

GREAT SPIRIT—Grant that I may not criticize my neighbor until I have walked a mile in his moccasins.

—*Indian Prayer*

WHEN THE CHILD says "I," it begins for the first time to see itself as if from the inside—it recognizes its own subjectivity of which it had not been aware before. Our experience of *ourselves* is utterly different from our experience or knowledge of another. We *cannot* know how life is, seems, feels, to another, in spite of the fact that at times it seems to us that we do feel things from the point of view of someone else. We say, for instance, that we see eye to eye with another, only to find out later that this has been an illusion, for the other has had all sorts of ideas and associations connected with the subject under discussion or the happening we have been experiencing together—ideas and associations that we have not shared at all. When an individual falls in love, he is convinced that the thoughts and feelings of the loved one are completely known, even identical with his own. He and she seem to be "soul mates," known to each other as though they were identical twins. But this, too, is an illusion. Nonetheless it is held as an ideal of love to "do unto others as ye would that they should do unto you," a command based on the principle of identification that by no means always produces the expected result. For individuals are exceedingly different, and what seems desirable to one may be quite the reverse to another. We *cannot* know how life is to another person; we are, every one of us, isolated in ourselves, "islands," forever alone. We may shrink from this realization, or we may glory in it, feeling ourselves to be different, stronger, more important than the others, who seem to us to be like mere automata. And so our "I" enlarges itself illegitimately.

—M. Esther Harding, *The 'I' and 'Not-I,'* p. 70

IN DAILY life it happens all the time that we presume that the psychology of other people is the same as ours. We suppose that what is pleasing or desirable to us is the same to others and that what seems bad to us must also seem bad to them. It is only recently that our courts of law have nerved themselves to admit the psychological relativity of guilt in pronouncing sentence. The tenet *quod licet Jovi non licet bovi* still rankles in the minds of all unsophisticated people; equality before the law is still a precious achievement. And we still attribute to the other fellow all the evil and inferior qualities that we do not like to recognize in ourselves, and therefore have to criticize and attack him, when all that has happened is that an inferior "soul" has emigrated from one person to another. The world is still full of *bêtes noires* and scapegoats, just as it formerly teemed with witches and werewolves.

—C. G. Jung, *Civilization in Transition,* Vol. 10 in Collected
Works, pp. 64–65, par. 130

A RELIABLE PROVING GROUND for our communication with each other at the nonverbal level would be the conscious practice of "experiencing the other side," the various roles those we regularly deal with—the other members of our families, the student body, the faculty, a deacon, a housewife—have to fulfill. When we do this, we catch basically ineffable apprehensions of the silent level of each other's being. We may have only a sentence with which to capture our venom as did Marc Connelly's character in *Green Pastures* who, seeing the crucifixion, said, "I guess being God ain't no bed of roses."

—Wayne E. Oates, *The Holy Spirit in Five Worlds*, p. 45

EXTERNAL considering means putting yourself in another person's position and realizing his or her difficulties. It is one way of *transforming* life. So now *become* the person you think has treated you badly or the person you are jealous of, etc. Try to do this sincerely. It requires a conscious effort. Visualize yourself as the person and reverse the position—that is, you become the person you dislike or hate or criticize, and you are now looking at another person, called yourself. As a rule this will cure you very quickly, if you can do it. But if you are in an evil state of negative emotion—as we all are at times—nothing will help you save realizing what you yourself are like—that is, what evil you have in you and what you are really like. This is painful. But we cannot change without pain.

—Maurice Nicoll, *Psychological Commentaries*, Vol. 1, p. 94

TO SENSE the client's inner world of private personal meanings as if it were your own, but without ever losing the "as if" quality, this is empathy, and this seems essential to a growth-promoting relationship. To sense his confusion or his timidity or his anger or his feeling of being treated unfairly as if it were your own, yet without your own uncertainty or fear or anger or suspicion getting bound up in it, this is the condition I am endeavoring to describe. . . . It is this kind of highly sensitive empathy which seems important in making it possible for a person to get close to himself and to learn, to change and develop. . . . I suspect that each of us has discovered that this kind of understanding is extremely rare. We neither receive it nor offer it with any great frequency. Instead we offer another type of understanding which is very different, such as "I understand what is wrong with you" or "I understand what makes you act that way." These are the types of understanding which we usually offer and receive—an evaluative understanding from the outside. It is not surprising that we shy away from true understanding. If I am truly open to the way life is experienced by another person—if I can take his world into mine—then I run the risk of seeing life in his way, of being changed myself, and we all resist change. So we tend to view this other person's world only in our terms, not in his. We analyze and evaluate it. We do not understand it. But when someone understands how it feels and seems to be me, without wanting to analyze me or judge me, then I can blossom and grow in that climate. I am sure I am not alone in that feeling. . . . None of us steadily achieves such a complete empathy as I have been trying to describe, any more than we achieve complete congruence, but there is no doubt that individuals can develop along this line.

> —Carl Rogers, *Person to Person: The Problem of Being Human,* pp. 92, 94

AGAIN, THIS MAN regards one day more highly than another, while that man regards all days alike. On such a point everyone should have reached conviction in his own mind. He who respects the day has the Lord in mind in doing so, and he who eats meat has the Lord in mind when he eats, since he gives thanks to God; and he who abstains has the Lord in mind no less, since he too gives thanks to God.

For no one of us lives, and equally no one of us dies, for himself alone. If we live, we live for the Lord; and if we die, we die for the Lord. Whether therefore we live or die, we belong to the Lord. This is why Christ died and came to life again, to establish his lordship over dead and living. You, sir, why do you pass judgment on your brother? And you, sir, why do you hold your brother in contempt? We shall all stand before God's tribunal. For Scripture says, "As I live, says the Lord, to me every knee shall bow and every tongue acknowledge God." So, you see, each of us will have to answer for himself.

Let us therefore cease judging one another, but rather make this simple judgment: that no obstacle or stumbling-block be placed in a brother's way.

                                         —Romans 14:5–13 (NEB)

WE DO not know the inmost depths of the human heart; it is revealed only to love. But those who condemn have generally little love, and therefore the mystery of the heart which they judge is closed to them. . . .

                          —Nicolas Berdyaev, *The Destiny of Man,* p. 109

AT DAYBREAK he appeared again in the temple, and all the people gathered round him. He had taken his seat and was engaged in teaching them when the doctors of the law and the Pharisees brought in a woman caught committing adultery. Making her stand out in the middle they said to him, "Master, this woman was caught in the very act of adultery. In the Law Moses has laid down that such women are to be stoned. What do you say about it?" They put the question as a test, hoping to frame a charge against him. Jesus bent down and wrote with his finger on the ground. When they continued to press their question he sat up straight and said, "That one of you who is faultless shall throw the first stone." Then once again he bent down and wrote on the ground. When they heard what he said, one by one they went away, the eldest first; and Jesus was left alone, with the woman still standing there. Jesus again sat up and said to the woman, "Where are they? Has no one condemned you?" She answered, "No one, sir." Jesus said, "Nor do I condemn you. You may go; do not sin again."

                                         —John 8:2–11 (NEB)

BE GENEROUS to one another, tender-hearted, forgiving one another as God in Christ forgave you.

                                         —Ephesians 4:32 (NEB)

PART THREE

CREATIVE SUFFERING

Suffering is too much a part of our days not to be deeply considered. It comes to every person. No one escapes, and yet so often the underlying feeling in us is that all should escape. We take sleeping pills, or vacations, or do the things which will bring relief before we have experienced the depth of our pain. We even use religion to flee and to help others take flight. Afraid to suffer, we nurture in ourselves the myth that it is our inalienable right not to suffer.

This does not imply that all suffering is to be embraced. There is no rule as clear as that. Only one guideline stands: suffering is not to be avoided, but overcome. Often it is in our resistance to suffering and in our struggle with it that we find whole new areas of freedom. There is a mental anguish which lets us know that we have violated something deep in us. It comes, as does physical pain, to tell us that all is not well. If we resigned ourselves to this kind of suffering, receiving it as our fate, we would not have heard its real message. It may be our very understanding of this, however, coupled with our fear of pain, which keeps us from recognizing that in the family of experiences there is a suffering which has a rightful place. It cannot be put out of the way. If we deny it the hours and even the weeks and months that it claims, our denial will make us ill. Defenses erected against suffering will stifle our lives and leave us with another kind of suffering, more painful than that which we sought to evade.

Unwillingness to experience the suffering which is ours to bear pushes it into the very deeps of us. This never deals with it. It finds its way back in a disguised form. That form may be an indefinable shadow over the future that fills us with dread. Or it may be that bitterness and anger become the signs of our refusal to give suffering an audience and to be taught by it. There is a suffering which we overcome by struggling with it, and there is a suffering which we overcome by acceptance. There are even some who argue that all suffering, to be overcome, must first be accepted, else we strike out blindly, missing the real point of engagement. If we are willing to experience our suffering, which is what is meant by acceptance, it will in turn allow us to go on to the claims of new feelings that belong to different hours. Ancient wisdom says there is "a time to weep."[1] It is the wisdom of Rachel:

> "A voice was heard in Ramah,
>   wailing and loud lamentation,
>   Rachel weeping for her children;
>   she refused to be consoled,
>   because they were no more."[2]

But what of the children of Rachel? When the heavens are deaf to the cries of children man asks an age-old question, "Does God live?" Can any consideration of suffering fail to ponder the children of Auschwitz and the children of Vietnam? Can we give sense to the senselessness of evil by saying that Rachel wrestled with the meaning of their death and found God? This takes no liberty with

1. Eccles. 3:4 (RSV).   2. Matt. 2:18 (RSV).

the substance of Scripture, for surely Rachel learned obedience and
spoke with an authority. With her stripes others were healed. We
can go this far with reasoning but then we are stopped. We cannot
deceive even ourselves into believing that the agony of the children
was in order that she might learn the things of God. Her love cries
another thing, "I could wish that I myself were accursed and cut
off from Christ for the sake of my brethren, my kinsmen by race."[3]
And we cannot forget all the Rachels who have looked up from the
butchering of their children to forever greet the world with a
blank, uncomprehending stare. Why does He who is Lord of history and of our histories, and who loves us utterly with no end to
His love, not send balm for our grievous wounds? Who will make
answer for the one he loves whose life is consumed by darkness and
whose soul "melts away for sorrow"?[4]

If I reply at all, it is simply to say that I believe, that I believe in
two worlds, and that one day there will be revealed all bare what is
only glimpsed now in a mirror darkly. But that is the witness of
faith. It does not come from outside oneself. It grows up inside,
cradled in the griefs of a hundred nights. If we live, we discover
that our suffering was also the seedbed of our faith.

The atheist and the agnostic will argue that they cannot position
themselves as men of faith because of the suffering they see about
them. And yet, it so often happens that when a man begins to believe in the inwardness of his being, it is because of his suffering.
It is hard to think about the eternal when all that one needs is
within reach. It is when all is lost that we ask from the center of
being the questions on which life hangs.

J. A. Sanders, professor of Old Testament at Union Seminary,
New York, in his speaking and writing[5] gives reminder that both
the Old and New Testament have their origin in the suffering of a
people. "The Torah as we now know it," he says, "was formed
out of the ashes of the first temple when all the outward symbols

3. Rom. 9:3 (RSV).   4. Ps. 119:28 (RSV).
5. J. A. Sanders, *The Old Testament in the Cross* (New York: Harper &
Row, 1961).

of promise were gone and a people in exile asked, 'Who are we? How do we live? What is our identity now?' "

The Torah, which means revelation or gospel, is the story that Israel told about itself and to itself in time of crisis—the story that is told when the crucial question is asked, "Who are we?" "We think," Sanders says, "that grace is being home in bed surrounded by friends, but grace is being out in the desert."

When I think about this I know that it is so. It is in the dark stretches that I find the doors to other rooms in myself. What is true for me is also true for others. I have a friend now who has walked all month in a black cloud. I want to help, but he does not want to be helped. He walks alone with himself and I am angry or jealous. I say to whoever will listen, "He likes to suffer." But even while I say it, I know it can be a lie as well as truth. It is a mistake to be enticed in too soon from desert places. We see there what we cannot see in the ordinary circumstances of life. It may be for this reason and for our own sake that we are instructed to visit the sick.

The sick in their suffering are closer to what is real. They see the things that really matter and are for a time in possession of different values. Sometimes they say out loud, "When I am well I will use my life to bind the wounds of the hurt." It is the same with desert suffering. Desert sufferers get in on the pain of the world and are like the sick in hospitals; they make resolutions as to how they will live when they are in life again. The difficulty is that the sick in bed and the sick in heart do not have the power to do what they think about, and when they are well again and walk by still waters, they have forgotten. Perhaps if we kept more fully our desert watches—stayed longer where the pain is—we would be different when we left the wilderness. As it is, we often have learned very little and so are destined to suffer in the same ways again.

Out of the sufferings of a people came the writings of the Old Testament, and out of the travail of the young Church the New Testament. The One in whom the twelve had put their hope was dead. Again there were no outward signs to give assurance. In their sorrowing they recalled the words He had spoken and the things He had done. "Do you remember the time . . . ? Do you remember . . . ?" And they did remember. In their search for balm they recounted for each other the stories He had told and all the private conversations He had with each of them. With the bridegroom taken, the time of fasting had come. They had to do more than find the meaning in their suffering; they had to give it meaning, for in the end this is what we each must do. Driven to meditate on the crucial question of identity, they reflected on their lives and on His life, and became aware of a Presence. Through every scrap of remembered conversation new light broke. Words that they responded to with only a surface hearing sank deep in their ears. Jesus had known that this was the way it had to be. What a man sees and what he is told need soil in which to take root. "So you have sorrow now, but I will see you again and your hearts will rejoice, and no one will take your joy from you."[6]

How did those words come real for John? When did he pull apart from the company of friends to keep his own desert watch? Did all things tremble when there began to move in him the thought that it was more than words or deeds that was claiming him? The medium is the message—the message is the Man. Jesus had not only spoken the word. He *was* the Word! But where was the Word before the Man? How far back did Christianity go? Did memory present the Scripture, "In the beginning God created the heavens and the earth . . ."?[7] Did John see in one flashing atom of time that *now* was tied in with *then?* Had he grown all still inside when he lifted his hand to give the revelation its language: "In the beginning was the Word. . . . All things were made through him, and without him was not anything made that was made."[8]

The transforming dimension of suffering is more easily traced in the life of Peter. He puts down his nets and leaves all to follow

6. John 16:22 (RSV).   7. Gen. 1:1 (RSV).
8. John 1:1, 3 (RSV).

Jesus, but faith remains something external to him. When the Master is present he can walk on water. In His absence he is again at the mercy of the dark waters that well up within him. The struggle of Jesus is to make the disciples aware that He has His power because of a relationship with the Father. It is a relationship that they can share in. His words always point them to the One who sent Him. The emphasis on the "sent" is so strong in the Gospel of John that when one begins to hear it the repetition is almost monotonous. It is closely linked with the statement, "I know where I come from, and where I am going."[9] He is telling them in one way or another, "My teaching is not really Mine, but comes from the One Who sent Me. . . . A man who speaks on his own authority has an eye for his own reputation. But the man who is considering the glory of God Who sent him is a *true man* [italics mine]."[10]

Peter does not become a man of faith by watching miracles. Christ heals the sick and feeds the hungry and raises the dead, but in each new situation the disciples must be shown again as though it had never happened.

And they discussed it among themselves, saying, "We brought no bread." But Jesus, aware of this, said, "O men of little faith, why do you discuss among yourselves the fact that you have no bread? Do you not yet perceive? Do you not remember the five loaves of the five thousand, and how many baskets you gathered? Or the seven loaves of the four thousand, and how many baskets you gathered?"[11]

The disciples were not privileged persons, as we sometimes think, living at a privileged place and time in history. They learned faith as most of us must learn it. The miracles and the stories become clear as the disciples are compelled from within to meditate on them. Faith begins in Peter as he suffers the knowledge that he is a man who can and does betray. It grows in him as he moves in the loss of the One that he loved more than any other. Faith becomes his as he dares to frame for himself the question he had once so impulsively answered, "Who was this Jesus?" When Peter

9. John 8:14 (NEB).   10. John 7:14 (Phillips).
11. Matt. 16:7–10 (RSV).

answers that question again it is Pentecost, and it is clear that the one speaking has become, like his Lord, a *true man*.

But Peter, standing with the eleven, lifted up his voice and addressed them. . . . "Let all the house of Israel therefore know assuredly that God has made him both Lord and Christ, this Jesus whom you crucified."[12]

The Old and New Testament are the words, stories, and prayers of men who suffer. They do not try to hide the fact that they suffer. They find suffering integral to life. They resist it, petition God to remove it, question it, endure it, rebel against it, accept it. As they wrestle with their suffering they find they wrestle with their Lord. Something happens to them—something as radical as new birth. The burden of their message does not become suffering but change—transformation. The news that they want to let the world hear about is the message of their Lord: "The only thing that counts is new creation!"[13]

It is the writer of Hebrews who tells us all we need to know: "He learned obedience through what he suffered."[14] The disciples do not prove greater than the Master. Neither will we prove greater than our Lord. If suffering is not itself the teacher, it is what makes us seek a teacher. Once I was told, and believed it, that somewhere it is written that he who seeks a teacher finds one. Suffering has the possibility of stabbing us awake. It shakes us out of accustomed ways so that we see ourselves as we are, powerless to change, yet needing change. But how does it come, this "new" that we must have?

Suffering can drive us deep into ourselves where, not on the surface of our lives, but at the center of being we ask the question, "Who am I? From where do I come and where am I going?" He who asks these questions stands in the way of receiving an answer. Suffering has the possibility of showing us the One that we have heard of. "I had heard of thee by the hearing of the ear, but now my eye sees thee. . . ."[15] Suffering has the possibility of enabling

12. Acts 2:14, 36 (RSV).   13. Gal. 6:15 (NEB).
14. Heb. 5:8 (RSV).   15. Job 42:5 (RSV).

us to bring all of our many selves under the Lordship of the Father. A power comes to those who are under this authority. They themselves become persons of authority. They possess themselves. This is their sonship with the Father. No authority in the external structures of the world can take away the authority of such persons.

Here and there in history stands a man who has learned obedience by what he has suffered. This is an age that might well note such a one, for there is everywhere rebellion against anyone who gives hint of having authority. In one way this has the sound of health. Deep in us we know that we need to be centered in ourselves—to make our own decisions, determine our own goals, suffer our own pain. The difficulty is that our lost authority is not recovered by protesting the authority of those in the outward order. Rebellion against authority today is more than rebellion against dehumanizing structures. It is right that the forces of oppression be confronted with a liberating spirit of rebellion. But contemporary rebellion is as much a quest for inner authority as it is a quest for external authority. Only one who has possession of himself with a true sense of inner authority can completely give himself to those who suffer under oppressive authority.

When the prison doors closed on Bonhoeffer, he looked through bars still a free man. One reads his prison letters and knows that, under the strict guard of his captors, obeying their every order, this man knelt before another Authority, and kept dominion over what he surveyed. On the way to the scaffold he was creating his own life and engaged in the creation of the world, exercising up until death the gifts of love and forgiveness—"Do not fear those who kill the body, and after that have no more that they can do."[16]

Jesus spoke as a man with authority. It is not an authority that we can give to ourselves. It is handed down from above to those who have learned obedience. This is what the centurion recognized. He knew instinctively that Jesus was a man under authority. He himself operated within a well-defined power structure. He was obedient to those above him and in turn knew what it was to have

16. Luke 12:4 (RSV).

others responding to his authority: "I'm a man under authority myself, and I have soldiers under me. I can say to one man, 'Go,' and I know he'll go. I can say to my slave, 'Do this,' and he'll always do it." It is because the centurion understands that the source of Jesus' power is a relationship with someone higher than Himself that Jesus says of him what seem like extravagant words, "Not even in Israel have I found such faith."[17]

The authority for which we truly hunger no one can take from us. We can only give it away ourselves. We give it to books and newspapers, to those whose good favor is important to us. More often we confer on internal moods the power to rule us—to afflict us with misery, to keep us imprisoned and fearful, seeking security. One day pain awakens us to our wretched lot. We know that we have lost self, but instead of turning home to God the Father, we scream at bewildered parents, the police, the man on the corner, and anyone with the outrageous thought that he can tell us what to do. The rage is appropriate in that it is a heinous crime to have been cheated out of one's birthright. The difficulty is that authority is not recovered in this way. The thieves who came in the night and stole our treasure are hiding out in our own souls. Our failure to deal with them there means that we project their images indiscriminately over the landscape and try to recover from a thousand persons authority which does not belong to us and would do us little good if we had it.

What we seek is a gift given to those who have learned obedience. It is conferred from on high and experienced within. When a man possesses it, he is free in two worlds—the world without and the world within. Moods and emotions that would hold sway and tyrannize lose their power. When the real authority is at the center of our lives we can say to one "Go!"—and to another "Come!" We are heirs then to all worlds and the Scripture is fulfilled.

When we have considered the suffering which is, as it were, our fate, there are yet other kinds of suffering to look at. Perhaps hardest

17. Matt. 8:10 (RSV).

to understand, but central to Christianity, is voluntary suffering. This is the cross that one is willing to take up in order to engage in the creation of his own life and in the creation of the world. Sometimes it comes in the form of anxiety that is experienced when an unknown way is chosen above the sure and familiar, or it may be the isolation that the prophet consciously moves into when he is aware that he speaks what the community does not wish to hear. In wartime it is the suffering of men who are prisoners in their own lands because of loyalty to an inner truth which conflicts with the course of governments. There is much suffering like this in our own country and other countries today. We live in times of such anger and surging unrest that it is uncertain what the internal struggles of our own nation will be and what it will mean to be in the fray for justice and not to flee the cities.

Yet there is something else about these times. We have grown aware that the terrible imbalances that exist in society also exist in our very beings. We have not been able to avoid seeing the feat of men on the moon against the plight of our urban centers. Every walk in moon dust illuminates in a piercing way the division and strife of earth men. We know that we have grown up lopsided. The age of the Spirit did not dawn with the age of science and technology, and the gap between the two threatens us and our kind with extinction. We possess the heights of the sky and the depths of the ocean, but the heights and depths within are unexplored. So long as this is true we are not in possession of ourselves. Much of our violence is the rage of the dispossessed, though it may be more appropriate to say the "have nots," for many of us never did possess ourselves. We are simply the deprived who have not claimed our inheritance to use either foolishly or wisely. Everywhere the recognition breaks with new force that the unexplored, untouched shores are within.

Each month one reads from another expert another fresh statistic which says that we are living at only 10 per cent of our creative potential—7 per cent—5 per cent. Some behavioral scientists are beginning to say they believe it is even less than 5 per cent. Driven by the pain of our self-estrangement and by promises held out of something better, there is on the part of thousands an anxious scramble to try to move into the land "all flowing with milk and honey." Institutes are springing up dedicated to helping participants feel, experience, and discover their real selves. There are thousands of other efforts on a smaller scale. Encounter groups, growth workshops, and sensitivity labs are conducted in basements, churches, and coffee houses, while motels are pushed into service as conference centers. Historians may well look back on these times and give their attention not to man in quest of other planets, but man in quest of himself. While the search has never been absent from any decade, it has not been pursued before by such great numbers and with so much intensity. For a few it is a quiet quest, for most it is more urgent. One person who was asked by friends to say what she had gained from a weekend workshop, simply said, "With me, it is a matter of survival." Survival is a word that is frequently used to describe the meaning of the personal encounter groups for participants.

Though by and large the Church has not known how integral the search for self is to the search for God, her saints have always preached that the two are inextricably bound together. Brother Lawrence is reported to have said, "When we enter upon the spiritual life, we should consider and examine to the bottom what we are."[18] In the fourteenth century, the author of *The Cloud of Unknowing* wrote, "Labor and sweat, therefore, in every way that you can, seeking to obtain for yourself a true knowledge and feeling of yourself as you are; and then I believe that soon afterward you will have a true knowledge and feeling of God as He is."[19] The conversations and teachings of Jesus are directed to the uncovering of a person's darkness, so that he can reach to the wellsprings of being. This is the reason for the harsh attack on the Pharisees.

18. Brother Lawrence, *Practice of the Presence of God* (Cincinnati, Ohio, Forward Movement Press), p. 19.
19. Anonymous, *The Cloud of Unknowing.* Introduction and translation by Ira Progoff (Julian Press, Inc., 1957), p. 94.

They have no feeling of themselves. Their lives are built on ex-
ternals, and Jesus in an effort to awaken them to their true state
uses a direct, stark approach which sounds very much like that prac-
ticed in some groups which have worked successfully with drug
addicts. A drastic kind of confrontation was needed, if they were
to be shocked into taking a look at themselves: "Woe to you,
scribes and Pharisees, hypocrites! for you are like whitewashed
tombs, which outwardly appear beautiful, but within they are full
of dead men's bones and all uncleanness."[20] It is a gentler Jesus who
talks with the woman of Samaria, but no less a confronting Jesus.
The woman who leaves Him feels known—"He told me everything that I ever did."[21]

In the controversial *Gospel according to Thomas*[22] is the reported
saying of Jesus:

> The kingdom is within you,
>   and it is without you,
> If you will come to know yourselves,
>   then you will be known by yourselves,
>   and you will understand that
>   you are sons of the Living Father.

Four hundred years ago in the opening sentences of the *Institutes
of the Christian Religion,* John Calvin wrote:

Our wisdom, in so far as it ought to be deemed true and solid wisdom,
consists almost entirely of two parts: the knowledge of God and of ourselves. But as these are connected together by many ties, it is not easy to
determine which of the two precedes, and gives birth to the other.

The secular context in which depth psychology developed pushed
the Church further toward making a separation of knowlege of self
and of God. Psychoanalysis separated the two, and the churches,
which never had them very well integrated, followed suit. It almost
seems as though the Church, fearful of the revelations of psychoanalysis, let the infant science convince her that self-knowledge and

20. Matt. 23:27 (RSV).   21. John 4:39 (NEB).
22. New York: Harper & Row, 1959, p. 3.

God were not of a piece. In accepting this message the Church was rejecting her own leaders. True, churches today have pastoral counseling programs, but for the most part it is hard to find any difference in these services from those offered in other counseling centers. They seldom call on the resources that are the Church's unique gifts. Self-knowledge is not seen as a quest that will help us see our true condition and bring us into that relationship with God in which the real self can be discovered.

Unless the Church can recover her own heritage—steep herself deep in the teachings of her own masters—she will have no word or ministry to a sick society. This means first to get deep in her own life the teachings that knowledge of God and ourselves are indissolubly related—that indeed they are connected by so many ties that we do not know which precedes and gives birth to the other. If we who are the Church can get that rooted in our feeling and thought processes, we will be able to celebrate and use in our pilgrimage all the findings of psychologists and anthropologists and behaviorists and anyone else who has a worthy tool to offer. For the business of knowing self is the business of the Church, and the fact that we have neglected it accounts in no small measure for the discrepancy between what the Church proclaims in her pulpits and what she lives out in her structures. The Church has not been true to the essential nature of her calling. She is cut off and is experiencing the most serious of all generation gaps. She has failed to find the saints contemporary. The tracks of men upon the moon were the work of generations of men. Our age has been able to build on the discoveries of mind that our fathers gave us, but the discoveries of the Spirit lie unused in books.

This brings us to the second teaching that the Church needs to discover anew. It is that the way is arduous. It leads, as Bunyan wrote from his prison cell, through the Slough of Despond. And the neighbors who will seek to keep one from the journey are numerous, and one's inner enemies more numerous still. It will never be made without a guide and faithful friend. At least once in every decade we might read *Pilgrim's Progress* again in order to understand better where each of us is in his own journeying. It might help to close the painful generation gap between ourselves and our fathers, which very likely has created the one between us and our sons.

Our fathers in the life of the Spirit say that what is required for our wholeness is sacrifice, discipline, a day-by-day taking up of one's cross. One wonders if the mystics would smile or turn away to see the leaders of sensitivity-awareness groups sending adults into the out-of-doors to find a piece of nature to contemplate for fifteen minutes. It is not that the experience is not a good one, but simply that participants in these workshops may never have it again unless they go to another workshop. There is a poignancy in what seems like the exaggerated response of grown-ups to simple exercises of touch and sight. Surely it speaks to us about the loss of wonder and the ache for its recovery. But if we become at all serious about heightened awareness we will have to listen again to the mystics, who say that if we are really to experience life through our senses as well as our intellect and emotion, we must set aside time each day for the training and disciplining of attention. We are learning that we have lost wonder, but we do not know yet that denial and labor are bound up in its recovery. Indigenous to our disease is the belief that even wonder and the possession of self are available at bargain prices.

If the Church could return to herself, she could speak the unpopular word that the way is arduous. But the Church in her efforts to be contemporary has also become separated from her center, and is saying nothing to the questing millions who want to be able to survive the turmoil and pollution of their own inner environments, and whose very search raises hope for the new age of the Spirit.

Perhaps the sufferings of the Church today will take her into her own desert experience, in which there will come a unifying of those four dimensions of her corporate existence which have become severed from each other. These are the dimensions of community, self, God, and world. Church leaders who involve themselves in trying to lead a people in developing these four sides of the corporate life of the Church are walking into suffering they could avoid if they would sacrifice their hope for the Church. Corporate structures, like individuals, have grown up weighted on one side. One congregation has its emphasis on prayer groups and Bible study, another on involvement in the problems of the city. The leader who works for some kind of balance between the two within the same congregation will have to handle problems of resistance and hostility within the group and within himself that would never surface if things were left as they are and everyone followed his own natural bias. When the other two dimensions are introduced, the pain and conflict is further intensified. Except for the Spirit no one would take on this kind of suffering. And yet, it is upon the unity of its various dimensions that the renewal of the Church in our time depends. All of these aspects of the Church have been covered separately by others in many volumes. It is their interrelatedness I want to stress, and the conviction that all four are essential to any movement toward wholeness. It is a conviction that persuades me that the Church is the primary institution for change. If there can be a healing of the division within its own inner life, it will be able to speak again of the "new man" and being "born again," for the fact is that the Church is the one institution which has as integral to its life the unity of all four dimensions. I comment on them briefly.

1. *The dimension of community.*   The Church when it is true to its own nature describes itself as a people—the people of God, the people of the New Covenant, the people of the Way. It is a community conscious of its past, its present, and its journeying toward a point in time when it will all end, and begin again in Christ. It is a community where the gifts of each person are called forth and celebrated and used for the upbuilding of the life of the entire community, whose corporate work is transformation.

Modern psychology has made us aware that we become individuals in relationship with others, and that where there is no genuine community the self is damaged and grows in crooked ways. We did not need the experts to tell us that. We have only to read our own biographies. This is what some of us did recently in my church community. We worked on Exercise 11 in this unit on suffering. Each wrote his own biography or odyssey and shared it in small group meetings. So many of our stories witnessed to the absence of community in the family and a human longing to be truly seen and heard, a craving that all too often went unheeded. One line in a biography which held as much human misery as any read, "I was taught to think that our family was slightly superior to other families and that I was slightly superior." It was surprising how many answering chords those words struck in others. As surprising was the high place given here and there to a grandmother. Occasionally a significant person had been a teacher or a neighbor, but over and over the figure recurred of the grandmother who had given to a child memories that continued to strengthen and sustain the adult. I wished that all Sunday-school teachers, grandmothers, aunts, uncles, and neighbors could have heard. Most of us would be better friends to small children if we knew how much it mattered. As it is we are not certain we are needed, or time is too short. We have lost faith that the small spaces of time we have for children can have impact, so we fill even these with nothing.

The one who teaches me most about these things is a little girl in one of the group homes the FLOC[23] program has established. The parents in this home are two women in their thirties. Together they are being mothers to five children whose own parents have abandoned them. In addition to their foster mothers each child in this home has an adult in the larger church community who is a friend or "uncle" or godmother. The child that is mine to shepherd knows more than most of us do about the importance of family. In the beginning I would simply introduce her to friends by name, but when she got the opportunity she would whisper a shy request, "Please tell them that you are my godmother." When she was thirteen, I said to her, "Now that you are a teen-ager, perhaps you would like to drop the 'aunt' and just call me by my name." "Oh

23. For Love of Children, an ecumenical program to reunite broken families and establish homes for homeless children.

no," she said, "I want to call you 'aunt.' Someone might believe it."

Her most serious question came, as all her serious questions do, in the midst of having fun, for play invokes in her, as it does in me, remembrance of sadder worlds. This time she asked, "If Mommy Dorothy and Mommy Bobbie were killed in an automobile accident, would you take care of me?" Satisfied with my answer, she was able to broaden her concern and ask, "Would you take care of all of us?" Assured again, she leaned back and said, "That sure is good, because I would hate to go back to Junior Village." Her concern then widened again, "But we will pray nothing happens to Mommy Dorothy and Mommy Bobbie."

One can simply say that this is the conversation of a child who has been left too many times, but the fact is that, while her fears may be more exaggerated than is ordinary, the strain of them runs in us all. They come within sight when we think what life would be like without the special one, or when we leap ahead in time to old age and wonder if there will be anyone there who cares. Of course, fears of abandonment are markedly reinforced for the child in households where there are insecure and overprotective adults or warring parents. But even in normal family units the child's security is increased if the family is in close relationship with others. In a talk in which Dr. Konrad Lorenz (of Max Planck Institute in Bavaria) stressed that large family groupings were essential to the survival of human society, he said of the family limited to two children and a father and mother, "The young child must know more than two people that are friendly. Because if you have just two people who are your friends—that 'we' are only four and the rest are 'they'—then 'we' are in a frightening minority."

The need of adults today for community—perhaps because of the lack of it in childhood—is as great as that of children. There are too many lonely and wistful family units to permit the belief that a community of one's children is sufficient. Sadder still are those small family units who do indeed believe they are sufficient. It is not only the child's hidden capacities and hungers that are uncovered and tended in community, but also those of the adult. Even when we do not know this with our conscious selves, we know it at the feeling level. We know it in our experience of deadness and the wistful hope that something will raise us up to life, or we know it in our restless quest for what we cannot name but must have, to fill our emptiness.

Today the hunger for a place in community is as urgent as the hunger to know self. And yet, we can travel the length and breadth of this land and find only here and there an experiment in community where persons have a life together and are consciously on the pilgrimage toward personhood, freedom, and responsibility. If we are looking for such a place, our pain is sometimes only intensified. We then interpret our suffering as an indication of our own capacity to be persons in deep relationship when it might more accurately be read as a sign of the void created by the absence of any meaningful existence with others. The community which we hunger for we are unable to create or to enter into; in subtle ways we manage to destroy what we say we want.

When the Church wakes again it will know that there can be no consequential change in the lives of people unless there is community. Perhaps then it will be able to issue once more the call that will enable each of us to reach down for the bits of ourselves—the widow's mite—that we can give to the building of the Church, which is to say the building of communities. No one will be able to say in advance what these communities will be like. That will depend on the resources of those who respond. It will be a call to come and labor, and suffer, and take risks in order to have the structures in which we can again be on a journey. If such a call were sounded, it might reach to the "pads" in cities and along shores where the young are carving out their new structures, too frail for gale and storm, but reminders nonetheless that we must build for meeting.

2. *The dimension of self.* Repentance and confession have always had as their base an understanding of the potentials for good and evil in each of us. The early Church was vividly aware that there could be no movement toward wholeness unless man

dealt with his own darkness; explicit in its teachings was the exhortation to deal with sin. The later shift to a more intellectual view of man made sin sound old-fashioned. Houses of prayer became houses of respectability, led by colorless men who lacked passion because—could it be?—their energies were being used to repress unacceptable feelings in themselves, the revealing of which would make them doubt their own leadership. In congregations where judgmental murmurings of, "But that is not Christian!" may be the response to one's confession, the climate is destroyed for exploring who we really are and discovering the feelings that lie beneath those with which we are familiar. Energy that might have been used to tap our own hidden resources must now be employed to protect one's dark side from discovery. When we are made to feel guilty for our feelings, then we begin to have a stake in not recognizing them in ourselves, and so begins the trek toward estrangement. Not only do we lose touch with our darkness but with its opposite, our so-called "goodness."

Recently a television reporter was interviewing shoppers and inquiring as to their hopes for the seventies. One soldier, seeming to ignore the question, seized the opportunity to say, "I was eighteen months in the Army with a former German citizen. I really gave him a rough time. I kept asking him how the Germans could explain the concentration camps. I said over and over, 'How could you do it?' All those eighteen months I made things hard for him. And now these past weeks I have been reading about My Lai and looking at the pictures, and I want to say to him, just in case he may be watching somewhere, 'Please forgive me!' "

For brief seconds the television camera had focused on a man still shaken with the discovery not only of his own shadow, but the shadow of America. Shadow is Carl Jung's term to describe those negative or undesirable qualities in ourselves that we have repressed so that we are not aware of them. They live, nonetheless, in a separate and infamous underworld from which they make wild forays into every realm of life. There they are labeled the enemy, and they strike back at those selves in us who in their struggle for purity and nobility have denied any association with these dark selves.

We can no longer afford to be ignorant of our shadow. I feel rather uneasy saying this, for it is the common knowledge of the Church, known since the Fall. There would seem to be little reason to repeat what we all know, but something tells me that this is illusion. I meet many people in their fifties who are in group therapy programs and are discovering for the first time that the friends they see on Sunday morning who appear so gracious and confident are seething cauldrons of fearful and hostile feelings. They are surprised to find that others know envy and greed and have selves that care little for the things of God. To be sure, we all have also an intellectual "I" which has gathered a store of information from scores of books on depth psychology. But it is an intellectual self with only a partial grasp of those other selves who are much more primitive, and believe that the way to deal with evil is to stamp it under foot and ignore its voice when it calls. They prevent darkness from emerging into light and coming under the Word of God.

It was said of Jesus, "He himself knew what was in man."[24] He knew the light and He knew the darkness, and that man, for wholeness, must keep a fateful encounter with both. One time He said, "Why do you call me good? No one is good but God alone."[25] It is the task of each person to discover his own darkness and his own light, and the primary task of the Church is to help in these discoveries. The very existence of man on this planet may be dependent on it. The world has grown too small and its arsenals too large for us to be able to project our shadows outside ourselves. The hope for the seventies is that we can lose our innocence— look on good and evil in ourselves, and let the gates close forever on the Garden of man's youth. Only then can it be said of the world that it has come of age.

3. *The dimension of God.* How shall the Church speak again of this engagement? The evil we did not see has done the dividing

24. John 2:25 (RSV). 25. Luke 18:19 (RSV).

work of evil. In our own nation we are divided. Poverty groups compete with poverty groups and money designated for the poor does not reach the poor. Black and white, rich and poor, young and old range themselves in opposite camps, and all the while in our own hearts opposing forces clash.

Shall we rush to the tops of buildings and cry to the cities below, "Repent!" Shall we once more recite for modern man his transgressions, which broadcasters proclaim every day and the newspapers record every night? Is there any new way to say that the rivers grow foul and the fisherman will mourn and lament? How else is there to cry that the skies are black and tomorrow they cave in and crush the land? The lights will go out and the cars on the highways cease to move. How tell the cities, "Your fortified streets cannot protect you from the lion that rages at your gates. The barrels of your guns shall be bent back and fire into your bedrooms." Or are there other words that only the Church can speak?

Hear, Los Angeles, Chicago, and Dayton! You have forgotten the God of your salvation. Listen, Washington and Hartford! You have not remembered the Rock of your refuge. Miami of the glittering coast, San Francisco, town that was given a gleaming bay, Pittsburgh of the chimneys, and all cities wise in your own eyes and shrewd in your own sight, woe to you, for you know not the way of your Lord! And New York, city of my own youth, among whose lovers and betrayers I am, your sin is chiseled out on the walls of your skyscrapers. You made your promises gods and went whoring with them. On every rooftop, under every bright light, you have played the harlot.

Has the Church any swift messengers to send to the cities . . . to a nation increasing each day her stockpile of weapons? Where are the Church's messengers

> to a nation, tall and smooth,
> to a people feared near and far,
> a nation mighty and conquering,
> whose land the rivers divide?[26]

26. Isa. 18:2 (RSV).

No one goes from the churches. In the churches we no longer hear God speak. It is the minister who addresses us, and he does not claim communion with God. He walks in more humble ways. There is no chance that he will succumb to the arrogance of those who claim to have been to the mountaintop and to have seen a vision. The last clergyman who said this we tracked down in the night and killed. Now there is no voice reaching across dividing walls to disturb us in our prejudices, and when the Sunday service is over we can return to our homes and live safe. No one will recognize and point out that we have been with Jesus. No one will notice in us a style of life different from his neighbor's.

It would seem unnecessary to say anything to the churches about the dimension of God, but it is again illusion to think that only the world has grown godless. The Church has so merged with the culture of the times that it is hard to distinguish what is said by her representatives from what is said by the representatives of any other institution. One of the disciplines of the task groups in my church is that members will be faithful in their daily intercessory prayer for one another. That might seem like an elementary requirement for church groups to make, so to be taken for granted that it would hardly warrant any emphasis, but the fact is that it keeps many in the church from joining these groups, as does the discipline of fifteen minutes of prayer each day and fifteen minutes of meditation. Small wonder the young are looking to the East for their teachers! It is not rebellion in the churches, but disbelief in a personal, transcendent God who drenches His people with healing, and empowers, and sends.

If the Church in its own desert experience should meet itself, it will know again that men are not fully human unless they are men in God. When the Church turns home to its Lord, and its people pray and fast and wait for the descending Spirit, perhaps the cities will be saved, for they languish not only for water, but holy water; not only for light, but holy light; not only for bread, but holy bread.

4. *The dimension of world.*   It is not enough for the Church to

exist for those who find their way into her life. This is wholeness for no one, for wholeness begins in an understanding of what the whole is. So long as we are concerned only for the little family in which we move and the little group we call our group, we are stunted in growth—pygmy men and women with no real understanding of truths which fundamentally affect our existence.

The first of these truths is that all of humanity is one. Just as many diverse members function as parts of the total human body, so every person and every segment of the human race is part of the total human body. We first see this truth working out in our own bodies. We see how pain in one little tooth or one little toe claims the energy and attention of all the other parts. Sometimes the whole body has to lie down and tend, as it were, the needs of one afflicted member. It is like that with the Church, says Paul. When one part suffers all suffer. No part can say to another, "I have no need of you . . . for by one Spirit we were all baptized into one body—Jews or Greeks, slaves or free—and all were made to drink of one Spirit."[27] Sometimes we are fortunate enough to see the interrelation of all the parts in larger units like the family, the church, and the school, but what also happens is that we merge our lives with these larger groupings. We try to increase ourselves by membership in them. They become extensions of ourselves, so that we are threatened when they are threatened.

We have a belonging to the larger community, but it is a belonging without separateness, and when this happens there is no individuality. There is only the mass mind and the mass response. In genuine community separateness is maintained. In genuine community we do not merge with the other. We come to see the other and reach across the space that is there between us. If we succeed in meeting, then that is communion. When we leave off communing we are not less than who we were, we are more. Where there is communion there is always some of the rapturous wonder of belonging to the whole of mankind, baptized into one body. To

27. 1 Cor. 12:21, 13 (RSV).

forget this, or ignore it, or never to know it, is not to be a *true man*. It is to remain in dwarfed condition.

The second truth is that God in the fullness of time betrothed Himself to all of mankind. He pledged Himself to stay with every person, race, and nation until each comes into its own uniqueness and its own fullness. This means that when any individual is oppressed, when any person anywhere suffers or fails to realize his gifts and potentials, then God in His Son suffers in that individual. If God in Jesus Christ has betrothed Himself to the whole human race, it is also true—and makes sense—that if any segment of humanity is cut off, God suffers in that segment even though it be our most frightful enemy.

A third corollary truth is that no part of humanity can come fully into its own until every segment comes into its own. Growth in persons is the capacity to see this; the local church which is true to itself is going to embody these truths in its very structures, so that in concrete form its people are up against what the church proclaims. It has to be this way. Talk seldom changes anyone. We are not changed by what other people tell us, or by what we tell to others. It is the multiplicity of selves that limits our hearing. One self proclaims a truth that other selves know nothing about and will wildly protest when they get their time on the stage. If those other selves are also to be brought under the unifying action of the Spirit, then they have to be exposed and challenged. They need to be routed out of their resting places, and for this the Church needs structures of involvement.

What I am saying is perhaps illustrated by my own experience in one of the task forces of our church, which was concerned with the sufferings of the children of Vietnam. I was in that group because of that self in me which affirms the truths I have just outlined. But when the group began to do more than talk and began actually to make plans to bring some of the wounded children of Vietnam to this country, another self with a whole different set of feelings moved into ascendancy. I felt myself growing afraid. Our number was only eight. The costs promised to be astronomical. We had to make a lifetime commitment to the children because we could not know whether a year later they would have any future in Vietnam. For the first time I looked around the room at my group members and wondered how trustworthy they were. How well were they acquainted with their other selves, who might in the hour of crisis beg retreat? More than this, I was no longer sure it was the thing for us to do. What difference could it possibly make to pluck out of this suffering country two of its children to save— and could they be saved? If their bodies healed, would their minds and spirits heal? Would we not do better to spend our efforts and money in another way? My late and timid questions were quickly answered and set aside by this group, but they were not answered in me. I was carried along where I would never have gone alone. I was a limping member of that group. It could not be otherwise. There were too many fearful I's in me demanding attention.

Then the first two children arrived. I saw them only a half-dozen times. One was the night they arrived, small and dying, at Andrews Air Force Base, but still able to reach out pencil-thin arms to take a toy. A member of our sponsoring group, who was one of their doctors at Children's Hospital, gave us a day-by-day report of their struggle with pain and their struggle to live. We prayed and watched over them, and before the month was out I knew that God had spoken true when he assured us that the hairs of our heads are numbered, for we had indeed counted the hairs of their heads. Months later I was driving one little boy to a tutoring lesson, and he kept repeating in childish delight, "Tomorrow is Halloween!" Because he knew almost no English words he pantomimed what this meant and laughed when I laughed. In his laughing were all the sermons that I had ever heard on how humanity is one, and all those different I's in me bowed down together in one amen.

Real growth in a person's life is not possible without awareness and acceptance of these four dimensions. The Church in the New Testament embodied them in its very life forms. It was a Church which turned back the encompassing clouds of darkness with a call to life and a call to come and be made new. But when one speaks of a Church whose structures are for transformation, then one has a Church which again must talk of sacrifice and denial and suffering, for these are what create this kind of Church and this is how change takes place. This is how we win through to the joy that the New Testament is talking about. "We are God's heirs and Christ's fellow-heirs, if we share his sufferings now."[28]

And so it is that when we have considered all kinds of suffering, we must say yes or no to voluntary suffering, for it is to us that the question is addressed: "Are you able to drink the cup that I drink . . . ?"[29] It is upon our answer that the future of the Church depends, if not the future of mankind. The question is difficult to hear, for the whole current of our age carries us in other directions. The modern interpretation of Jesus Christ as the "man for others" swallows up the deeper one of Jesus Christ as the suffering servant. We scarcely understand the question He asks, for in the end we know that our lives must be the response. Martin Luther King, leaving the sanctuary of his church and setting his face toward Memphis, carried in his being the central message of Christianity.

The message of voluntary suffering is especially difficult to grasp in a psychological age that has an intellectual awareness of the sufferings that drain its life. We have all been made conscious of a neurotic style of life in which the sufferer clings to his suffering. It may be a strong wind at his back, but it holds him up when he leans against it, and he is not quite certain what there is to put in its place. Perhaps in rare moments some of us have entertained the idea that we may be the architects of our own suffering. Though for the most part we would reject such a thought as absurd, we are nonetheless afraid enough of masochism in ourselves to put the emphasis on self-fulfillment and the actualization of one's potential. This is as it should be so long as we can become aware that the process requires us to give up one kind of suffering and take on another kind. In both acts there is a cross. The evolution of a man and the evolution of a world will always involve that cross. We

28. Rom. 8:17 (NEB).   29. Mark 10:38 (RSV).

must suffer in the realization of ourselves, and we must suffer if we participate in the world's realization of itself. Any one who looks deeply into his own life finds out that it is, after all, not by mistake that Scripture ties joy to suffering in the same sentence: "Jesus . . . Who for the joy that was set before him endured the cross. . . ."[30]

The section on suffering that follows has been broken down into five exercises so that we can look more fully at suffering in our lives. Actually there are no sharp divisions between them. They simply enable us to look at suffering from a number of different perspectives. Sometimes the readings in one exercise could have been used as effectively in others.

Exercise 7 is concerned with the suffering that comes to each of us because we are born, and walk this earth, and must leave it. It is the suffering which is ours because we are human and belong to a human family and therefore are vulnerable. It is unlike suffering which we have the power to change and which comes to let us know that we have violated what is fundamental to our being fully human. In this first exercise we are concerned with the suffering we must allow to be the cross on which we are stretched, so that its redemptive work may be done.

Exercise 8 focuses on the suffering we know because life does not turn out as we thought it would. We imagined how things would be for us, and this is good. Imagination is an essential ingredient of hope. It enables us to reach out for what we see and to develop our gifts and to make plans and have dreams. But when these plans and dreams are not realized, or do not work out according to our expectation, there comes a time when we need to give them up so that God can give us new plans and dreams. If we cling then to the old and review in our minds what might have been, we keep a gnawing sense of unfulfillment and resentment, a hungering for what cannot be. This may have been the experience of Judas. He did not grasp the concept of the Messiah as the suffering servant and, like so many in his day, clung to old political expectations of

30. Heb. 12:2 (RSV).

how the Kingdom should be ushered in. For his disappointment and holding to the old, he could not perceive and enter into the new.

Exercise 9 continues this work. It is another way of looking at the suffering we know because we have refused to say Yes to what is. We experience life as unfair and the world as hostile because they do not give us what we think is our just due. Whereas Exercise 7 is concerned with our learning how to experience unavoidable suffering, so that we are deepened by it, the next two exercises both deal with the suffering we must give up because it narrows and restricts our lives. To hold to suffering past its season is to have an idolatry in one's life.

Exercise 10 concerns voluntary suffering. This is the suffering we could avoid, but willingly take on because we know it is necessary to our own wholeness. There are convictions that we will have to suffer for, if we are not to betray ourselves. There is a certain aloneness and isolation that we will enter into, if we are to find that which is real in us. There is a cross which all men take up when they are faithful to the mission of loving. It may hurt to love, but those who take on suffering know that it hurts more not to love.

Common to all these exercises is acceptance. The unavoidable pain must eventually be accepted, if it is to do its transforming work. We must accept the unfulfilled expectations that home and culture have nurtured in us, as well as the deprivation we know when our deepest yearnings are blocked. Without this acceptance we become frozen in the past—unable to look to the future. Finally, we must accept and not fear the suffering we intuitively know to be a part of the adventure of not holding back and therefore living our lives fully.

The last exercise is the writing of one's autobiography. We are asked to take time out to reflect on our own history to see how events and our response to them have made us who we are.

EXERCISE 7

Choose what is an area of suffering for you

Identify what is an area of suffering for you, and seek to embrace
it. Try to rest in the suffering, affirming by faith that God is using
it to form your heart and spirit. Think what it means to be a co-
creator with God in this work.

Practice five minutes of recollection before reading the material
in any of the exercises. This will enable the words to reach to
deeper places in you. Then read slowly and meditatively. As you
read, try to be aware of selves in you which resist what you read
and which do not like the whole idea of embracing suffering. Be in
dialogue with these selves. Their opinions are more important to
you than the ones you meet on the printed page. That rebellious
self may need more instruction than your peaceful assenting self,
but on the other hand you may find it a good teacher and guide.

HUMBLE YOURSELVES therefore under the mighty hand of God, that in due time he may exalt you. Cast all your anxieties on him, for he cares about you. Be sober, be watchful. Your adversary the devil prowls around like a roaring lion, seeking some one to devour. Resist him, firm in your faith, knowing that the same experience of suffering is required of your brotherhood throughout the world. And after you have suffered a little while, the God of all grace, who has called you to his eternal glory in Christ, will himself restore, establish, and strengthen you.

—1 Peter 5:6–10 (RSV)

THE FUNDAMENTAL END of human existence, as far as Christians are concerned, is that we come into living, personal relationship with that Center of Consciousness Who holds the universe in being. If God is, and we are his creatures, then to be in covenant relationship with him is what life is all about. It is a matter of being spoken to by a living Thou who is concerned equally for all of humanity, and whose anger is aroused when any segment of his people is abused or deprived. It is to hear from his own being what our place in salvation history is because he has told us where to be and what to do. In the Judeo-Christian tradition we are called to be in relationship with a God who can actually penetrate our lives, who can impinge upon us, who can speak to us, who can act on us and to whom we can respond. It is to be delighted by him, it is to rejoice in him, it is to anticipate his judgment, it is to look to completion and fulfillment and ecstasy as a result of union with him. The God of the Bible is a God who speaks to man in history. This is elementary, but it needs to be said because our age is having difficulty believing God calls us each by name.

Our task is to become awakened so that we are men and women normally in dialogue with the Living God. We can know this God and hear his address to us, but only when our wills are pliant, yielded and responsive—obedient to the acting, initiating will of the Father. We cannot know a sense of presence when we set ourselves over against him or when we conceive ourselves to be the initiating center. Jeremiah, whose prayers are a conversation with God, put it this way:

> I know, O Lord, that the way of
>   man is not in himself,
>   that it is not in man who walks to
>   direct his steps.
> Correct me, O Lord, but in just
>   measure;
>   not in thy anger, lest thou bring
>   me to nothing.
>   —Jer. 10:23–24 (RSV)

The PROPHET perceived that he needed to yield himself to that which was higher in him, but he was wise enough to know that there is pain in learning to do this. He exercises caution in his petition lest God make it more than he can bear.

There are other deep hints in Scripture as to how one develops this yielded and pliant will which knows how to respond to the initiating Thou, but none so revealing as the passage of Hebrews which says that Jesus learned obedience through suffering.

Again and again we find in the writings of the early Christians that strange statement—"We rejoice in our sufferings." How peculiarly unmodern that is. So much of our energy is spent avoiding suffering. At the Christmas worship for the children I said two things which were paradoxical. I don't know whether the children understood or not, but it did not seem too early for them to begin to hear them. First I said that life gets better and better. It is much better to be a child than to be a baby. It is much better to be an adolescent than a child, much better to be a young adult than a teen-ager, and much better to be old than middle-aged. It would be wonderful, I told them, if we could learn this, and then we could move ahead and know that it is better to die, although we should not push this occasion—or any other stage of life. But life really gets better and better. The second thing I told the children was that life is rough. I think we really need to know this, because so much

of our time is spent avoiding the roughness—avoiding suffering.
But life brings with it suffering and we can spend our lives trying
to escape it, or we can welcome suffering as a teacher. What we
need to learn is that life is good in its roughness.

Suffering can be defined, at least one dimension of it, as that
which is a threat to my personal being at the level at which I now
live my life. It may be that we are living in circumstances that are
far from ideal. There is suffering in this. There is suffering which
comes from the indifference of friends—those who do not care.
There is a suffering which comes when we seek to be responsible—
to do the thing which is right and in the scheme of things for us
to do, and our efforts are blocked.

There is the betrayal of friends, which is one of the most difficult
forms of suffering. There is the suffering which comes from separation, the inability to make contact with another when you really
care. There is suffering when the one you thought would understand fails to understand. There is suffering which comes from the
hostility of people. Anyone who really cares and voluntarily takes
on people knows this kind of suffering.

There is a suffering which comes when you have a dream. A
Martin Luther King cries out, "I have a dream, I have a dream,"
and he thrills millions of people. But there is suffering for him
who has the dream and is not able to bring it to fulfillment and
holds it fast decade after decade.

There is suffering which comes from facing a dimension within
our lives of which hitherto we have been unconscious. It is the pain
of awareness.

There is the pain of anxiety when sudden illness strikes and uncertainty hangs over the future. There is that most terrible of suffering when we watch those we love suffer pain—sometimes over
agonizing years. Then there is the pain of caring for those whose
lives are bound and knowing that their sick choices mean that their
freedom grows smaller and smaller. And there is suffering which
comes when we begin to identify with all of humanity and come to
be aware at a new level of dehumanizing systems and institutions.

There are many kinds of suffering and the amazing thing the writer of Hebrews says is that Jesus learned obedience through suffering. It is a matter of not turning from it. No deep lessons are learned if we run from pain. The most tragic thing that can happen is that one can suffer all one's life and never know a higher level of life for it. From the perspective of the Christian faith, suffering can be a dear friend. Life is all about a moment-by-moment dialogue with a living Lord, but it is a yielded, perfected will than can know in depth this unbelievable covenant relationship. Without this school of suffering the will is not perfected. That which we most resist may be our greatest opportunity.

—From a sermon by N. Gordon Cosby

LIKEWISE THE SPIRIT helps us in our weakness; for we do not know how to pray as we ought, but the Spirit himself intercedes for us with sighs too deep for words. And he who searches the hearts of men knows what is the mind of the Spirit, because the Spirit intercedes for the saints according to the will of God.

—Romans 8:26–27 (RSV)

THE DOCTRINE OF ACCEPTANCE does not deny evil, or say that it is but a stage in the development of good. It claims that evil, although it is irrational, and cannot rationally be explained in a world where the only source of life is God, is nevertheless necessary to freedom. It is therefore necessary to any goodness which is not automatic, determined, and meaningless. It is most real, and not to be denied or belittled or confused with good, but accepted and conquered, *not by extermination but by absorption.*

. . . . .

The harvest of suffering cannot be reaped until it has been eaten, burnt, digested. If the suffering is accepted and lived *through,* not fought against and refused, then it is completed and becomes transmuted. It is absorbed, and having accomplished its work, it ceases to exist as suffering, and becomes part of our growing self.

. . . . .

. . . Though we may be willing to accept hardness for ourselves as the necessary price of our inheritance, we cannot bear to accept it for those beloved who tear our heart-strings. We are too soft-hearted, or faint-hearted, or perhaps too lacking in faith. Even after the pilgrim has lost his burden and won by the grace of God to the end of his pilgrimage, he still has his family anxieties! He has to learn that "we can do a wrong to our children by standing between them and danger," trying to protect them from the painful finding of their own salvation. Christian has passed over, with all the trumpets sounding, maybe, but still "he is always trying to have a carriage sent back from the Celestial City for Christiana and the children.[30] . . . It cannot be done. Every generation has its own perils, privileges and possibilities. We can only stand aside and "let be." Then they can "walk on."

Are we exaggerating? See how it works in concrete instances. "This child whom I so love is going wrong. I cannot bear it. She must be saved from herself, made good." "My friend is dying of cancer. I cannot bear his suffering. His pain must be removed." "I am terribly unhappy. I cannot bear my life. Something must be done to make me happy."

But in truth nothing can be done about any of these things until we have first accepted them, not in words but in reality. This will not mean that we grow indifferent to them: they must cause us extensive suffering. But it will mean that we are *willing* to suffer, and to learn what they may have to teach. Not only willingness for ourselves, but for those we love, whom we are so anxious to help by our favourite technique of refusal, exercised on their behalf.

—E. Graham Howe and L. Le Mesurier, *The Open Way,*
pp. 126, 180, 127–128

After this Job opened his mouth
and cursed the day of his birth.

30. From H. G. Wells, *The Soul of a Bishop.*

And Job said:
"Let the day perish wherein I was born,
    and the night which said,
    'A man-child is conceived.' "
Let that day be darkness!

    .   .   .   .   .

"Why is light given to him that is in misery,
    and life to the bitter in soul,
who long for death, but it comes not,
    and dig for it more than for hid treasures;
who rejoice exceedingly,
    and are glad, when they find the grave?
Why is light given to a man whose way is hid,
    whom God has hedged in?
For my sighing comes as my bread,
    and my groanings are poured out like water.
For the thing that I fear comes upon me,
    and what I dread befalls me.
I am not at ease, nor am I quiet;
    I have no rest; but trouble comes."
                              —Job 3:1–4, 20–26 (RSV)

BUT BEAR IN MIND: your sufferings might well be called useless, and that we men can certainly be tempted to speak of useless suffering as beyond the reach of comfort. But this is only human speech. In the language of eternity, the suffering that helped you to reach the highest is far from useless. Alas, it is only useless and unused when you will not let yourself be helped by it up to the highest. . . .
  —Søren Kierkegaard, *Purity of Heart Is to Will One Thing*,
                                             p. 154

WHEN RABBI SHMELKE and his brother visited the maggid of Mezritch, they asked him about the following. "Our sages said certain words which leave us no peace because we do not understand them. They are that men should praise and thank God for suffering just as much as for well-being, and receive it with the same joy. Will you tell us how we are to understand this, Rabbi?"

The maggid replied: "Go to the House of Study. There you will find Zusya smoking his pipe. He will give you the explanation." They went to the House of Study and put their question to Rabbi Zusya. He laughed. "You certainly have not come to the right man! Better go to someone else rather than to me, for I have never experienced suffering." But the two knew that, from the day he was born to this day, Rabbi Zusya's life had been a web of need and anguish. Then they knew what it was: to accept suffering with love.

—Martin Buber, *Tales of the Hasidim: Early Masters,*
pp. 237–238

EACH MAN BEARS a burden exactly like that of all others in this: it is just beyond his strength! The equality of men is there. There is prodigious fraternity in the human condition: everybody gasps under a weight which he is incapable of bearing. Each one experiences a fundamental powerlessness. Each one measures his nothingness. Each one learns, through his burden, what is that of all the others.

The mature man knows that the world is beautiful, the universe rich, existence varied and savory, and, at the same time, that life is impossible, that it has always been so, that it will always be so, and that one must not be merely man in order to face it.

Faith is this complement of reasons and forces without which our scale is forever unbalanced. . . .

.   .   .   .   .

What is unbearable is not to suffer but to be afraid of suffering. To endure a precise pain, a definite loss, a hunger for something one knows—this it is possible to bear. One can live with this pain. But in fear there is all the suffering of the world: to dread suffering is to suffer an infinite pain since one supposes it unbearable; it is to revolt against the universe, to lose one's place and one's rights in it, to become vulnerable over the whole extent of one's being.

—Louis Evely, *Suffering,* pp. 152, 153

THERE are ways of coming to know oneself that do not require lasting preoccupation with the self. There are ways of believing in oneself without making oneself the center of the universe. There are ways of accepting oneself without rejecting others. The wildness we might find in our deep selves is not necessarily our damnation. It may be necessary for our salvation. While many of us might think we are happy and complete, few of us ever achieve the kind of fullness that is possible only with and after a thoroughgoing exploration of our true selves. While a plant does not have to understand what it is to be a plant in order to be one, a human being can never be fully human unless he knows who and what he is. He comes to this understanding by knowing himself not only as angel but as animal. Some of his self-knowledge may not be satisfying, but self-satisfaction is not necessarily the goal or the result of self-searching. The self we ultimately come to know may be far less adequate than the self we would like to imagine we are. *While we may have to sacrifice far more or far less than we dream, in the process of coming to know and accept ourselves for what we are, we often fear most the loss of illusions rather than the true giving up of the self.*

We need such knowledge of our possibilities, unadorned with illusion, before we can ever really live. Certain values of society, and all too frequently of religion, tend to stupefy and anesthetize us. They teach us to avoid pain and sorrow, to deny anxiety. And we gladly, happily embrace this deception. We abdicate our true identity for a superimposed identity. But the superimposition doesn't take. The deception doesn't work. Pain and sorrow and anxiety find us anyway and we, anemic and unprepared, become ill and unhappy. In failing to explore ourselves. We have lost our armor against hardship.

—Earl A. Loomis, Jr., *The Self in Pilgrimage,* pp. 7–8

AND HOW DO WE know that we exist if we do not suffer, little or much? How can we turn upon ourselves, acquire reflective consciousness, save by suffering? When we enjoy ourselves we forget ourselves, forget that we exist; we pass over into another, an alien being, we alienate ourselves. And we become centered in ourselves again, we return to ourselves, only by suffering.

.   .   .   .   .

Our own struggle to acquire, preserve, and increase our own consciousness makes us discover in the endeavours and movements and revolutions of all things a struggle to acquire, preserve, and increase consciousness, to which everything tends. Beneath the actions of those most akin to myself, of my fellow-men, I feel—or, rather, I co-feel—a state of consciousness similar to that which lies beneath my own actions. On hearing my brother give a cry of pain, my own pain awakes and cries in the depth of my consciousness. And in the same way I feel the pain of animals, and the pain of a tree when one of its branches is being cut off, and I feel it most when my imagination is alive, for the imagination is the faculty of intuition, of inward vision.

—Miguel de Unamuno, *Tragic Sense of Life,* pp. 140, 141

"AND JOSEPH'S MASTER took him and put him into the prison, the place where the king's prisoners were confined . . . and the Lord was with Joseph." What is this God who goes to prison? Why doesn't he do what any decent self-respecting deity ought to do? Why doesn't he send a medium-sized earthquake to crumble the prison walls so that the hero can escape? A living God who solves people's problems, especially good people, would just blast the communists, I mean the Romans, I mean the Egyptians, off the map and save the good guy. Now that would be a god who does what a decent self-respecting god ought to do. Now that would be a god you could believe in. You wouldn't call him "dead"! But our poor text says that the biblical God was with Joseph in prison. What a sad, mixed-up Bible. And this is only Genesis. If it carries on like this, it's no telling where it'll end up. The next thing you know, it'll be trying to tell us that he was with the later Israelite slaves in Egypt, making bricks without straw. If this keeps up it'll be trying to tell us that God, too, was a P.O.W. with the Israelite prisoners in Babylon's dungeons during the Exile. And then the next you know, it'll probably want to say that when old Herod was killing all the baby boys who might threaten his realm, that God somehow got down into one of those cradles. And then you watch it, it'll end up with some tomfool story about how he got onto the cross of some teacher charged with blasphemy and sedition against the state. ". . . And he was there in prison, and the Lord was with Joseph."

—From "Joseph, Our Brother," a sermon by J. A. Sanders

THE MAN STRAPPED naked to a table and turned in all directions, even upside down, for a spinal myelitis examination, aware and in initial embarrassment because doctors and nurses are observing him, not only in his nakedness but especially in his very defense-lessness, comes to realize that what he has hidden (intellectually, mentally) was not really hidden. It is still there in his suffering body, and finally he has to face it; but simultaneously he has to recognize something far more important: those "strangers" who view his body and handle it, do so in the profound charity of a search for healing. No matter how physically and psychologically painful this may be, he can realize that those who help are lifted to charity through the pain that afflicts his body. For that amount of time, something tremendous and pure has occurred. And he may even feel the deep balm of a first understanding that the body, so denied in some of its aspects, so hated, perhaps, has longed for the same sunlight as the soul; and that in God's sight, if not in man's, there is no blushing, no turning away, no priorities in parts but a reality of the whole.

—John Howard Griffin, *Creative Suffering*, pp. 31–32

Excerpt from a letter written March 9, 1944:
THIS IS MY second passiontide here. People sometimes suggest in their letters that I am suffering here. Personally, I shrink from such a thought, for it seems a profanation of that word. These things mustn't be dramatized. I should not be at all surprised if you, and

indeed almost everyone else nowadays, are suffering more than I am. Of course, there's a good deal here that's appalling, but isn't it the same everywhere? Perhaps we have tended to exaggerate the whole question of suffering, and have been too solemn about it. I have often wondered before now why it is that Catholics take such little notice of this sort of thing. Is it because they are stronger than we are? Perhaps they know from their own history better than we do what real suffering and martyrdom are, and therefore they pass over petty inconveniences and obstacles in silence. I believe for instance that all real suffering contains an element of physical pain. We are always too much inclined to emphasize the sufferings of the soul. Yet that is just what Christ is supposed to have removed from us, and I cannot find anything in the New Testament about it, or in the acts of the early martyrs. There is all the difference in the world between the Church's own sufferings and the untoward experiences of one of her servants. I am sure we need a good deal of correction on this point. Frankly speaking, I sometimes feel almost ashamed to think how much we have talked about our own sufferings. Indeed, real suffering must be quite a different matter and have a quite different dimension, from anything I have experienced hitherto. Enough for today. When shall we be able to talk together again? Take care of yourself, and make the most of the beautiful country you are in. Spread *hilaritas* around you, and mind you keep it yourself!

—Dietrich Bonhoeffer, *Letters and Papers from Prison,*
pp. 146–147

THE NEW TESTAMENT everywhere insists that we can know the power of Christ's resurrection only if we also know the fellowship of His sufferings. If, without our choice or contrivance, feelings arise within us which cause distress, then Christ is there in the distress itself, not to save us from the pain of rebirth but to assure us that we are indeed being born again. To change the analogy: when, of old, there stirred in Abraham the desire to leave the city where he belonged and to travel he didn't know where, perhaps the most obvious course would have been to persuade him that he suffered from wanderlust—a disturbance of which God would cure him. And when, after a few months, the cure complete, he settled down contentedly once again in Ur of the Chaldees, you could have talked of Theotherapy. But Abraham would have lost everything—his vocation, his integrity, his soul. He would have been the victim of the cheap grace which is not grace.

—H. A. Williams, *The True Wilderness,* p. 41

BOTH BUDDHISM AND STOICISM are interesting because they recognize that existence is pain; Buddhism does it directly, Stoicism indirectly. The problem of the meaning of suffering is essential to ethics. It is the main theme of Christianity. Suffering is the inmost essence of being, the fundamental law of life. All that lives endures pain and suffering. In this respect pessimism is metaphysically right. All optimistic metaphysical systems are flat and superficial. But our attitude to life is not determined by the fact that life is pain and suffering. Pessimism is a false doctrine after all, because it is afraid of suffering, renounces existence, flees from the battlefield and betrays life. I may know that life is pain and at the same time accept life, accept its suffering and understand the meaning of it. This is what Christianity does, and it alone.

There are two kinds of suffering—the light and redeeming suffering which leads to life, and the dark and evil suffering which leads to death. A man may go through suffering serenely and graciously and be born into a new life as a result of it. All the sufferings sent to man—the death of his nearest and dearest, illness, poverty, humiliations and disappointments—may serve to purify, raise and regenerate him. But suffering may finally crush man, embitter him, destroy his vitality and make him feel that life has no meaning whatever. Nietzsche says that it is not so much the suffering as the senselessness of it that is unendurable. Man can go through the most terrible sufferings if he sees a meaning in them; human powers of endurance are enormous. Christianity gives meaning to suffering and makes it endurable. It gives meaning to it through the mystery

of the Cross. Man's suffering is twofold. He suffers from the trials
that are sent him, from the blows which fate deals him, from death,
illness, privations, treachery, solitude, disillusionment and so on,
and so on. And he suffers, too, from rebelling against suffering,
from refusing to bear it and from cursing it. And this is another
and a bitterer kind of suffering. When man accepts suffering and
recognizes that it has a meaning, the pain grows less, becomes more
endurable, and a light begins to shine through it. Unenlightened
suffering, the most terrible of all, is that which man does not
accept, against which he rebels and feels vindictive. But when he
accepts suffering as having a higher meaning, it regenerates him.
This is the meaning of the Cross. "Take up thy cross and follow
me." That means, "Accept suffering, understand its meaning and
bear it graciously. And if you are given your cross, do not compare
it with, and measure it against, other people's crosses." To try to
avoid suffering and run away from it is self-deception and one of
the greatest illusions of life. Suffering tracks our steps, even the
happiest of us. There is only one way open to man, the way of
light and regeneration—to accept suffering as the cross which everyone must bear following the Crucified. This is the deepest mystery
of Christianity and of Christian ethics. Suffering is bound up with
sin and evil, just as death is—the last of man's trials. But it is also
the way of redemption, of light and regeneration. Such is the
Christian paradox with regard to suffering and it must be accepted
and lived through. For a Christian to suffer means voluntarily to
take up and bear his cross. Compulsory suffering must be accepted
freely. Suffering is closely connected with freedom. To seek a life
in which there will be no more suffering is to seek a life in which
there will be no more freedom.

—Nicolas Berdyaev, *The Destiny of Man,* pp. 118–119

BLESSED BE THE GOD and Father of our Lord Jesus Christ, the
Father of mercies and God of all comforts, who comforts us in all
our affliction, so that we may be able to comfort those who are in
any affliction, with the comfort with which we ourselves are com-

forted by God. For as we share abundantly in Christ's sufferings, so through Christ we share abundantly in comfort too. If we are afflicted, it is for your comfort and salvation; and if we are comforted, it is for your comfort, which you experience when you patiently endure the same sufferings that we suffer. Our hope for you is unshaken; for we know that as you share in our sufferings, you will also share in our comfort.

For we do not want you to be ignorant, brethren, of the affliction we experienced in Asia; for we were so utterly, unbearably crushed that we despaired of life itself. Why, we felt that we had received the sentence of death; but that was to make us rely not on ourselves but on God who raises the dead; he delivered us from so deadly a peril, and he will deliver us; on him we have set our hope that he will deliver us again. You also must help us by prayer, so that many will give thanks on our behalf for the blessing granted us in answer to many prayers.

—2 Corinthians 1:3–11 (RSV)

AND WHAT OF OURSELVES? With all these witnesses to faith around us like a cloud, we must throw off every encumbrance, every sin to which we cling, and run with resolution the race for which we are entered, our eyes fixed on Jesus, on whom faith depends from start to finish: Jesus who, for the sake of the joy that lay ahead of him, endured the cross, making light of its disgrace, and has taken his seat at the right hand of the throne of God.

Think of him who submitted to such opposition from sinners: that will help you not to lose heart and grow faint. In your struggle against sin, you have not yet resisted to the point of shedding your blood. You have forgotten the text of Scripture which addresses you as sons and appeals to you in these words:

"My son, do not think lightly of the Lord's discipline,
   nor lose heart when he corrects you;
   for the Lord disciplines those whom he loves;
   he lays the rod on every son whom he asknowledges."

You must endure it as discipline: God is treating you as sons. Can anyone be a son, who is not disciplined by his father? If you escape the discipline in which all sons share, you must be bastards and no true sons. Again, we paid due respect to the earthly fathers who disciplined us; should we not submit even more readily to our spiritual Father, and so attain life? They disciplined us for this short life according to their lights; but he does so for our true welfare, so that we may share his holiness. Discipline, no doubt, is never pleasant; at the time it seems painful, but in the end it yields for those who have been trained by it the peaceful harvest of an honest life. Come, then, stiffen your drooping arms and shaking knees, and keep your steps from wavering. Then the disabled limb will not be put out of joint, but regain its former powers.

—Hebrews 12:1–13 (NEB)

I REMEMBER my dilemma in a concentration camp when faced with a man and a woman who were close to suicide; both had told me that they expected nothing more from life. I asked both my fellow prisoners whether the question was really what we expected from life. Was it not, rather, what life was expecting from us? I suggested that life was awaiting something from them.

. . . . .

But even a man who finds himself in the greatest distress, in which neither activity nor creativity can bring values to life, nor experience give meaning to it—even such a man can still give his life a meaning by the way he faces his fate, his distress. By taking his unavoidable suffering upon himself, he may yet realize values.

Thus, life has a meaning to the last breath. For the possibility of realizing values by the very attitude with which we face our unchangeable suffering—this possibility exists to the very last moment. I call such values *attitudinal values*. The right kind of suffering—facing your fate without flinching—is the highest achievement that has been granted to man.

I should like to illustrate my point by the following case. A nurse in my department suffered from a tumor which proved to be inoperable. In her despair the nurse asked me to visit her. Our con-

versation revealed that the cause of her despair was not so much her illness in itself as her incapacity to work. She had loved her profession above all else, and now she could no longer follow it. What should I say? Her situation was really hopeless; nevertheless, I tried to explain to her that to work eight or ten hours per day is no great thing—many people can do that. But to be as eager to work as she was, and so incapable of work, and yet not to despair —that would be an achievement few could attain. And then I asked her: "Are you not being unfair to all those thousands of sick people to whom you have dedicated your life; are you not being unfair to act now as if the life of an incurable invalid were without meaning? If you behave as if the meaning of our life consisted in being able to work so many hours a day, you take away from all sick people the right to live and the justification for their existence."
—Viktor E. Frankl, *The Doctor and the Soul,* pp. x–xi, xiii–xiv

"YOU ARE NO LONGER a child, Reuven," my father went on. "It is almost impossible to see the way your mind is growing. And your heart, too. Inductive logic, Freud, experimental psychology, mathematizing hypotheses, scientific study of the Talmud. Three years ago, you were still a child. You have become a small giant since the day Danny's ball struck your eye. You do not see it. But I see it. And it is a beautiful thing to see. So listen to what I am going to tell you." He paused for a moment, as if considering his next words carefully, then continued. "Human beings do not live forever, Reuven. We live less than the time it takes to blink an eye, if we measure our lives against eternity. So it may be asked what value is there to a human life. There is so much pain in the world. What does it mean to have to suffer so much if our lives are nothing more than the blink of an eye?" He paused again, his eyes misty now, then went on. "I learned a long time ago, Reuven, that a blink of an eye in itself is nothing. But the eye that blinks, *that* is something. A span of life is nothing. But the man who lives that span, *he* is something. He can fill that tiny span with meaning, so its quality is immeasurable though its quantity may be insignificant.

Do you understand what I am saying? A man must fill his life with meaning, meaning is not automatically given to life. It is hard work to fill one's life with meaning. *That* I do not think you understand yet. A life filled with meaning is worthy of rest. I want to be worthy of rest when I am no longer here. Do you understand what I am saying?"

—Chaim Potok, *The Chosen*, p. 204

MATURITY INVOLVES both acceptance and gratitude. Each man enters into life wounded, deformed, and graceless: parents injure their children with prejudice, fear, and carelessness; societies cripple minorities by injustice and hatred; nature brings to birth many of her children with defects and abnormalities. A central task each man faces in the formation of an identity is the acceptance of the deformities and limitations which are his destiny. Self-acceptance is the prelude to responsibility and creative change. Before we may be graceful we must accept our gracelessness. Mere acceptance and resignation, however, are not sufficient; gratitude is, finally, necessary to full integration and self-acceptance. Nietzsche remarked that a man must come to love his wounds. A sensitive analysis of the dynamics of human personality reveals that it is impossible to delete those deformities and limitations which we are all tempted to despise without completely altering the person. To accept and love the self is to come, gradually, to love the battles it has had to fight and the wounds it has sustained. Radical self-acceptance and integration require that we accept all that has made us what we are. To be grateful *that* we are involves gratitude for *what* has made us as we are. Thus, gratitude and forgiveness are both essential to wholeness. That resentment which causes us to despise our wounds and our limits is finally directed not at something that is accidental to our being but at our being itself. Gratitude alone allows us the freedom from our wounds and our past which is necessary for autonomous action. Gracefulness requires that, in the end, we become able to say of those events we are tempted to despise and reject: "In enduring them, I have become fuller and more authentic."

. . . . .

We must begin by acknowledging the inevitability of failure. There is no hope that we can eradicate evil and tragedy—only that we can find ways of keeping the spirit alive. This being the case, we must be able to speak of gratitude at the same time that we acknowledge the existence of evil. In fact, it is only when we set as a *norm* a model of life in which gratitude is appropriate that we have a standard by which to judge the measure of evil that man creates and suffers. We may judge as a violation of the sanctity of life all that makes gratitude and wonder more difficult or impossible. It is because we define gratitude as a condition of authentic life that we can resist all those concrete forms of injustice and evil that lead inevitably to bitterness and resentment. The tragedies of Auschwitz, Watts, and Vietnam have the stink of sacrilege precisely because they violate the hope and expectation each human being harbors that his life may achieve its potential fullness. Every man covets the opportunity to take the measure of his life and be able to pronounce the judgment, "It is good." And it is only to the degree that we are able to forge the diverse moments of pain and pleasure, emptiness and fullness, loneliness and love, and failure and success into some meaningful and gracious whole that we are able to escape that resentment and bitterness which form the roots of gnosticism, neurosis, and despair. Finally, the most significant index we have of the stature of a man is the amount of pain and tragedy he has been able to bear and still rejoice in the gift of life. We cannot make unambiguous life the conditions of gratitude; if we did, rejoicing and celebration could only be carried on where we ignore the tragic character of actual existence or be postponed until we reach Utopia or Apocalypse. We may (and, indeed, must) speak of the necessity for gratitude without being blind to all that conspires to deny each man his birthright of the possibility of graceful existence.

—Sam Keen, *Apology for Wonder,* pp. 207–208

EXERCISE 8

Discover an expectancy that gives you discontent

In your time of meditation try to discover an expectancy which you have held on to and which makes you discontented because life does not fulfill it. Perhaps it is only left over from yesterday, but it may be an expectancy which has been stored in you from childhood or youth. Try to be aware of times when it makes you unable to appreciate what life does give to you.

Each day practice accepting what the day brings that you have no control over—the visitor who throws your schedule off, the telephone call that interrupts your train of thought, the event that was not in your planning, all the green lights that turn red as you reach them.

If you are keeping a journal, note in it each night what you observe about yourself. Record, if you can, some of the dialogue between selves with conflicting feelings. There may be a self which feels that everyone should be aware of its needs and which lies on the floor and kicks its feet and screams when all does not go according to its plans, and there may be a scolding parent-self that says,

"How can you behave like that? Get yourself up off that floor."
And there may be another self standing in the background who can
extend an invitation, "You obviously would not be there, if you
knew of other choices. Come let us reason together."

IN YOUTH a person may identify with many intimate imaginings of what he or she is going to grow into, what position, what palace, they will possess, and how many servants and what chorus of praise and sympathy will surround them. These and similar imaginings can form very strong impressions. . . . The result will be that in growing up a sense of discontent or of disappointment, or a sadness, pervades the outlook, the cause being unknown to the person although it is still evident in the imagination. The tendency will be to look backwards because life as it is experienced will seem in some way unreal, the reason being that in view of the forms of expectancy laid down by the early imaginings the life is not what was expected. . . .

—Maurice Nicoll, *Psychological Commentaries,*
Vol. 3, pp. 839–840

YEARS ago I used to notice the differences among motormen on the Indiana Avenue streetcar line in Chicago—a street often blocked by badly parked cars and huge trailer trucks backing into warehouses and maneuvering in everybody's way. Some motormen seemed to expect to be able to drive down Indiana Avenue without interruption. Every time they got blocked, they would get steamed up with rage, clang their bells and lean out of their cars to shout at the truck drivers. At the end of a day these motormen must have been nervous wrecks; I can imagine them coming home at the end of the day, jittery and hypertensive, a menace to their wives and children. Other motormen, however, seemed to expect Indiana Avenue to be heavily blocked—a realistic expectation, because it usually was. They could sit and wait for minutes without impatience, calmly whistling a tune, cleaning their fingernails, or writing their reports. In other words, confronting the same objective situation, some motormen lived a hellish life of anger and nervous tension; other motormen had a nice, relaxing job, with plenty of time for rest.

—S. I. Hayakawa, *Symbol, Status, and Personality,* p. 81

ONE OF THE STRANGEST lessons that our unstable life-passage

teaches us is that the unwanted is often creative rather than de-
structive. No one wished to go to Weihsien camp. Yet such an
experience, resisted and abhorred, had within it the seeds of new
insight and thus of new life for many of us. Almost because of its
discomfort, its turmoil, and its boredom, it eventually became the
source of certainties and of convictions with which life could henceforth be more creatively faced. This is a common mystery of life,
an aspect, if you will, of common grace: out of apparent evil new
creativity can arise if the meanings and possibilities latent within
the new situation are grasped with courage and with faith.

This common experience—that the Fate which we did not welcome has become nevertheless the ground for future creativity—has,
more than anything else, led men to speak of the Providence of God
and to believe in His universal creative presence. I did not come to
believe that God determined all aspects of the events in which I
participated. But the experience of creativity in a circumstance
neither intended nor wanted, has led me to believe that God works
in and through each situation. And strangely, this divine activity
provides the possibility of a new departure, a more vivid life, and
a deeper joy than could have been provided by the life I had myself
intended.

—Langdon Gilkey, *Shantung Compound*, p. 242

BUT surely, it is the mark of a grown-up man, as compared with a
callow youth, that he finds his centre of gravity wherever he happens to be at the moment, and however much he longs for the
object of his desire, it cannot prevent him from staying at his post
and doing his duty? The adolescent is never quite "all there": if
he were, he wouldn't be an adolescent, but a dullard. There is a
wholeness about the fully grown man which makes him concen-
trate on the present moment. He may have unsatisfied desires, but
he always keeps them out of sight, and manages to master them
some way or other. And the more need he has of self-mastery, the
more confidence he will inspire among his comrades, especially the
younger ones, who are still on the road he has already travelled.

Clinging too much to our desires easily prevents us from being what we ought to be and can be. Desires repeatedly mastered for the sake of present duty make us, conversely, all the richer. To be without desire is a mark of poverty. At the moment I am surrounded by people who cling to their desires, so much so that they haven't any interest for others: they give up listening, and are incapable of loving their neighbor. I think we should live even in this place as though we had no desires and no future to hope for, and just be our true selves. It is remarkable what an influence one acquires in this way over other men. They come and confide in us, and let us speak to them. I am writing to you about this because I think there is a lot for you to do too just now, and later on you will be glad to think that you have done your best. When we know that a friend is in danger, we somehow want to be assured that he is being his true self. We can have a full life even when we haven't got everything we want—that is what I am really trying to say. Forgive me for troubling you with my thoughts, but thinking is my chief amusement here. I'm sure you'll understand. I ought to add, by the way, that I am more convinced than ever that it won't be long before *our* wishes are fulfilled, and there's no need for *us* to resign ourselves to the worst.

—Dietrich Bonhoeffer, *Letters and Papers from Prison,*
pp. 148–149

THEY SEIZED PAUL and Silas and dragged them into the market place before the rulers; and when they had brought them to the magistrates they said, "These men are Jews and they are disturbing our city. They advocate customs which it is not lawful for us Romans to accept or practice." The crowd joined in attacking them; and the magistrates tore the garments off them and gave orders to beat them with rods. And when they had inflicted many blows upon them, they threw them into prison, charging the jailer to keep them safely. Having received this charge, he put them into the inner prison and fastened their feet in the stocks.

But about midnight Paul and Silas were praying and singing

hymns to God, and the prisoners were listening to them, and suddenly there was a great earthquake, so that the foundations of the prison were shaken; and immediately all the doors were opened and every one's fetters were unfastened. When the jailer woke and saw that the prison doors were open, he drew his sword and was about to kill himself, supposing that the prisoners had escaped. But Paul cried with a loud voice, "Do not harm yourself, for we are all here." And he called for lights and rushed in, and trembling with fear he fell down before Paul and Silas, and brought them out and said, "Men, what must I do to be saved?" And they said, "Believe in the Lord Jesus, and you will be saved, you and your household." And they spoke the word of the Lord to him and to all that were in his house. And he took them the same hour of the night, and washed their wounds, and he was baptized at once, with all his family. Then he brought them up into his house, and set food before them; and he rejoiced with all his household that he had believed in God.

—Acts 16:19–34 (RSV)

WE EXPECT too much of the world. Our expectations are extravagant in the precise dictionary sense of the word—"going beyond the limits of reason or moderation." They are excessive.

When we pick up our newspaper at breakfast, we expect—we even demand—that it bring us momentous events since the night before. We turn on the car radio as we drive to work and expect "news" to have occurred since the morning newspaper went to press. Returning in the evening, we expect our house not only to shelter us, to keep us warm in winter and cool in summer, but to relax us, to dignify us, to encompass us with soft music and interesting hobbies, to be a playground, a theater, and a bar. We expect our two-week vacation to be romantic, exotic, cheap, and effortless. We expect a faraway atmosphere if we go to a nearby place; and we expect everything to be relaxing, sanitary, and Americanized if we go to a faraway place. We expect new heroes every season, a literary masterpiece every month, a dramatic spectacular every week, a rare sensation every night. We expect everybody to feel free to disagree, yet we expect everybody to be loyal, not to rock the boat or take the Fifth Amendment. We expect everybody to believe deeply in his religion, yet not to think less of others for not be- lieving. We expect our nation to be strong and great and vast and varied and prepared for every challenge; yet we expect our "national purpose" to be clear and simple, something that gives direction to the lives of nearly two hundred million people and yet can be bought in a paperback at the corner drugstore for a dollar.

We expect anything and everything. We expect the contradictory and the impossible. We expect compact cars which are spacious; luxurious cars which are economical. We expect to be rich and charitable, powerful and merciful, active and reflective, kind and competitive. We expect to be inspired by mediocre appeals for "excellence," to be made literate by illiterate appeals for literacy. We expect to eat and stay thin, to be constantly on the move and ever more neighborly, to go to a "church of our choice" and yet feel its guiding power over us. To revere God and to be God.

Never have a people been more the masters of their environment. Yet never has a people felt more deceived and disappointed. For never has a people expected so much more than the world could offer.

—Daniel J. Boorstin, *The Image, or What Happened to the American Dream,* pp. 3–4

MOST potent are the ghosts of the unlived past—ghosts of the things one did not do, commitments one did not make, choosing instead the provisional life that did not demand decisive choice. These ghosts haunt the crossroads, reiterating that it is too late, or too soon, or not possible now; but when "God takes you and cleans away all your ghosts," you accept the here and now and try to see what you can make of your life in spite of limitations and past mistakes. Then you can "step out on the waves" and "come back to live all over again."

You come back to the same old life; but the old is now the new

because a new concept reanimates and transforms it. Now when
you journey on the waves, you understand that these waters are
waters of life: you see beneath the surface the deeper forces moving. The fantasies, the dreams, the visions, the intuitions of truth
that arise within you are no longer ghost whispers blowing through
you as wailing or singing wind blows through a windharp; they are
real living experiences that speak their meaning in both inner and
outer life. The voice we now hear is that of the Living Word that
moves upon the waters of life. Good and evil are realities, and we
accept the burden of choice.

— Frances G. Wickes, *The Inner World of Choice,* p. 15

THROUGH OUR CONTEMPLATIVE expectation of God, we enter into
those acts of acceptance which are necessary every day; acceptance
of our situation in life, of our growing old, of lost opportunities,
and of failures. Regret itself is transformed into a positive act,
repentance, which gives new power to our movement forward.

In *Thomas Gordeieff,* Gorki tells of how Ignatius' boat is destroyed by ice on the Volga. Although a miser and watching every
rouble, he at once accepts this loss. He realizes that regrets would
be in vain, and already begins to reassure himself with the thought
of building a new boat.

In regret, the inner man disintegrates. The human spirit, far
from being invigorated, becomes sterile when it drags itself through
thoughts which uselessly reconstruct a bygone situation.

There are some childhoods which are invitations to an unconscious remorse. One always wants to start all over again in order to do
better. But what work is there that we do really well? We always
move in the realm of the pretty near. Regrets kill the creative impulse. Regrets are debilitating. If we are given a moment of certainty, of security, a sure standing ground, it is when we come
together to wait upon God. Then everything becomes possible
again, the salt regains its savour, that which had grown insipid
acquires a wholly new meaning.

In contemplative expectation of God, all the pessimism which clings to us is dissolved, even if this pessimism has valid reasons for being there in what we see of the contemporary world and of ourselves.

There are so many reasons for pessimism in the world. There are those ever-growing masses of people, deprived of the sense of God, and those Christian societies turned in on themselves, which in Europe have known centuries of fratricidal strife. There is the prospect in twenty years' time of seeing four thousand million undeveloped people, as against one thousand million well-fed. There is that immense wave which is slowly breaking over us: a technological civilization which encompasses man and totally submerges him.

There are also many inner motives for discouragement: the struggle which we carry on day by day, the old self who will not submit, that pride of life, that hardness of will which refuses to take account of our neighbour, that despondency of fatigue. So many reasons for pessimism in our lives!

In contemplative expectation of God, all things become desirable again. Pessimism is dissolved and gives way to the optimism of faith. Then alone is it possible to appreciate what is coming to us, to welcome the events which today brings us, to hasten towards our neighbour, to set out afresh, to press forward. Only in contemplative expectation of God can we recover our lost impetus.

—Roger Schultz, *The Power of the Provisional,* pp. 76–78

EXERCISE 9

Observe self-pity in yourself

It is easy to be aware of self-pity in others. It is much more difficult to observe it in ourselves, even though it eats away at our very life, and this is what self-pity does. It is a particularly pernicious form of suffering and uses up energy that might otherwise be used for creating ourselves and our world. One way of identifying self-pity is by being alert to hear the words or the feeling, "if only." "If only I had married the right person. If only I had a child. If only my child had been born healthy. . . ." Behind an "if only" there can be an area of real suffering and real deprivation, but it is a suffering that we have failed to accept, and continue to use our strength in rebellion against, so the "if only" sounds with a large "poor me" refrain which keeps us impaled.

The task this week is to observe self-pity in yourself and, whenever you do observe it, to practice turning your attention to an area of your life situation where change is possible. If such an area does not readily present itself, it will be important to spend time discovering those places of freedom where you can exercise dominion and participate in creation.

NOTE: The Scripture from Genesis may at first glance seem unrelated to our task and subject. It contains, however, the authoritative command to subdue the earth. It is about a creating God and man made in His image—man still finite, but born to be a creator and *have dominion*. This state is the opposite of self-pity, for self-pity indicates that man has come under the domination of events and circumstances. Instead of being in control, he is controlled. Instead of being able to say to the work of his hands and mind and spirit, "It is good," he feels himself to be helpless and the victim of life.

Then God said, "Let us make man in our image, after our likeness; and let them have dominion over the fish of the sea, and over the birds of the air, and over the cattle, and over all the earth, and over every creeping thing that creeps upon the earth." . . . And God said, "Behold, I have given you every plant yielding seed which is upon the face of all the earth, and every tree with seed in its fruit; you shall have them for food. And to every beast of the earth, and to every bird of the air, and to everything that creeps on the earth, everything that has the breath of life, I have given every green plant for food." And it was so. And God saw everything that he had made, and behold, it was very good. And there was evening and there was morning, a sixth day.

—Genesis 1:26–31 (RSV)

SO ALSO IN MY OWN personal history, I should endeavor to learn the precious lesson which Israel's sacred writers teach me: To love whatever I find. Actually there is no other reaction to the happenings of my life that makes sense. Any other reaction will only rob me of the possibility of becoming truly human. It is this attitude of faith which alone can keep me truly a member of the human race. The secret is simply to love what I find. It is the open-hearted attitude towards all the eventualities of my earthly existence which alone can ultimately bring me true fulfillment. "He who sows in sorrow and in tears shall come back bearing his sheaves with joy."
          —David M. Stanley, *A Modern Scriptural Approach to the*
                                        Spiritual Exercises, p. 56

ON OCCASION, profound lessons come from unusual sources.

The following is a verbatim transcription of a therapeutic interview with a blind child. The child was not allowed to continue in school because he was said to be "out of touch with reality."

This is a record the patient did not know was being taken—the pure, stark expression of a brilliant soul struggling to find itself.

Here is what the therapist says of the patient:

"Bob is 12 years old. He has been blind since birth. He is a bright boy, eagerly interested in the wonders of the world around him—a world that he has experienced in his own way, but has never seen. He is interested in science—especially electronics. He reads everything he can get under his curious fingertips. Bob has great potential. He is sensitive, intellectually gifted far beyond his years—and he desperately wants to find his place in the world."

In Bob's own words, here are some of the things he wonders about and believes in:

"There are so many things in this world, that people could all reach out and touch and keep a part of them for their very own and spread it around for everyone. Not money—because money is only good for what it can do—only good if it is used to help. But people could reach out for kindness and fair play—and could spread it around for others.

"I've heard on the radio all this talk about integration in the schools. To give all children a chance to go to school together. And there seems to be such a fuss about it because some of the children are different. And I can't understand at all what this great difference is.

"They say it's their color. And what is color? I guess I am lucky that I cannot see differences in color because it seems to me that the kind of hate these people put in their minds must chase out all chance to grow in understanding."

Another time he had this to say: "I noticed the other day when I had an earache and had cotton in one of my ears, that I was always veering to one side and bumping into the wall. I had not realized before how much I depend on my hearing—the sound of my steps, the bounce-back of the sound, to keep me in time with my sense of direction.

"Then, another time, I was walking down the hall and I passed a door and inside that other room was a lot of noise. So much noise that I lost all my cues—and I lost completely my sense of direction.

"It was an awful, bottomless feeling. Afraid I'd bump into something. You never know whether you are going toward good things or toward trouble. Because you never know right off if it is something you like and need and want. Or something that is just in the way.

"That is why I would not kick it, or blame it, or shove it aside. I would not make up my mind ahead of time, because if I did I could be so very wrong. I could destroy something that might be one of the most important and valuable aids to me. Destroy it in ignorance. Without giving either it or me a chance. That's like prejudice."

Another time he talked about the problem of keeping a sense of direction:

"I walked down the path toward the woods by the school. And all of a sudden a dog and another boy rushed by. They threw a branch of a tree in front of me. I was startled and I jumped back and fell into some bushes. When I untangled myself and got up on my feet I couldn't find the path. I couldn't tell which direction was which. I couldn't hear any telltale sounds as a guide.

"I called. Nobody answered. I was surrounded by silence and confusion. Then after a lot of trying and a lot of falls and scratches and bumps into the bushes, I heard the chimes on the old church that is north of the school. I knew then where I was. And I got back all right. But that awful feeling of not knowing where I was, which way to turn, which way to go. It was a terrible feeling.

"And suddenly I thought of Campy [Roy Campanella, former Brooklyn Dodger catcher]. All of a sudden he finds himself paralyzed. All his life suddenly has to change. He can't turn around any more. He can't even walk.

"I asked myself would I rather be blind like I am or would I rather be flat on my back and paralyzed like Campy. I thought about it for a long, long time. I thought of how I felt when I fell in the bushes and couldn't tell where I was. I thought of the panicky fear when I didn't know which way to turn. I was asking myself which was worse. I always said there wasn't anything worse than being blind. Then I thought of Campy again.

"He had been a great ball player, one of the greatest. Now all of a sudden that was over. What was he thinking about now? Probably wondering what he would do now. Probably wondering which way he would turn. And I decided the worst thing that can happen to a person isn't being blind or being paralyzed. The worst thing is to lose all sense of direction in your life. And feel that you haven't got any place to go."

Bob talked about his blindness one day. "I have often wondered what it must be like to see. I have never seen light. But if I have darkness around me all the time, I must learn to know that darkness. I think I do know it very well. Sometimes as a friend. Sometimes as an enemy.

"But then it isn't the darkness that I should blame. Because darkness can be either friend or enemy. If wishes could come true, I'd wish I could see. But if I only had one wish, I wouldn't waste it on wishing I could see. I'd wish instead that everybody could understand one another and how a person feels inside."

While endless debates go on in high places and political jockeying for position is the order of the day, here is the simple solution to the basic problem this confused strife-worn world faces in this New Year.

—Howard A. Rusk, M.D., "Light in Darkness,"
in *The New York Times,* January 4, 1959

THIS FACULTY TO ACT at once on two planes can be dissipated when it becomes merely an attempt to escape an awareness of pain. No, it must be the contrary—an acceptance and an awareness of the reality that exists in pain and that sometimes becomes obsessive in pain, and then a growing ability, from the same root, to stand off and become the observer; and then again, passing on to the observation of other things until at length and in the natural order of things, the observing self comes to the realization that self, even in pain, is less interesting than other objects of contemplation. It is this realization, which takes time, that ultimately liberates the sufferer: not from his suffering, no; not from an acute awareness of his suffering, no; but from the otherwise exclusive, obsessive, paralyzing, sterilizing enslavement of suffering.

This begins to occur, for example, when the man who is deprived of some freedom by pain—perhaps the freedom to walk—is initially overwhelmed by the deprivation: absorbed in the deprivation or the pain; then, as he learns, as he lives with it, the interest is less sustained. He can see the person not thus deprived climb steps without any hesitancy and feel some unwholeness because he cannot do that; but then he can begin to see that simple act which to him is now impossible no longer as a reproach to himself, no longer as a reminder of his own deprivation. But in the light of that, from the same root, as a marvelous sight, he sees the man bounding up steps as something extraordinary, beautiful; he sees and marvels at the freedom and lack of pain and concern in the man climbing the steps, and this rather than his own inability is far more interesting.

He watches, and feels a kind of joy that others can do this marvelous thing. He watches it the way others might watch a great athlete,
or a dancer like Nureyev: not in self-loathing because few men are
great athletes or have the skills of a Nureyev, but because of the
beauty of those who have these gifts.
                    —John Howard Griffin, *Creative Suffering*, p. 27

DIFFICULTY IN ACCEPTING the given is often obvious and easily
understandable, but it sometimes assumes a subtly disguised form.
Reluctance to face the facts sometimes appears as an artless inability
to recognize the given for what it is, a failure to understand that
some of the unpalatable conditions facing us must *be* faced before
we can proceed.

This failure springs from a deceptively credulous effort to ex-
pand the limited activity known as hypothetical thinking into a
form of complete living, an "if, then" sort of existence: If things
were a little different; if my nose were not so big; if my parents
were not so poor; if I hadn't made the mistake of marrying Henry
(instead of ending the marriage or making something of it). How
much better the whole prospect would be if some of the details
were different! And why couldn't they have been different?

This way of looking at things, when expressed baldly in such
terms of wistful wishfulness, is incredibly naïve. And yet, talk of
this kind is heard all the time. Moreover, this same response to the
given is often made by means that are much more subtle and in-
direct; we have some extremely sophisticated ways of crippling ourselves by rejecting the presented terms upon which we must achieve
psychic existence if it is to be achieved at all.

                    .   .   .   .   .

The recognition that some elements and aspects of the given
cannot be changed may lead us toward the view that the given as a
whole is unchangeable. This is the conclusion reached by some
people. It appears to us, however, that there are usually some parts
of any particular given world which can be changed, manipulated,
rearranged. There is *almost* always an area of freedom available

to everyone. This area may be large or small. Even though it be so small that it can hardly be detected, it is usually there. And in most cases it is probably large enough to have some significance. Moreover, the use made of an area of freedom does not depend entirely on its size. Some ingenious people have done remarkable things in a mere sliver of maneuvering space.

—Raymond Rogers, *Coming into Existence:*
The Struggle to Become an Individual, pp. 20–21, 18

THOSE PRISONERS who blocked out neither heart nor reason, neither feelings nor perception, but kept informed of their inner attitudes even when they could hardly ever afford to act on them, those prisoners survived and came to understand the conditions they lived under. They also came to realize what they had not perceived before; that they still retained the last, if not the greatest, of human freedoms: to choose their own attitude in any given circumstance. Prisoners who understood this fully, came to know that this, and only this, formed the crucial difference between retaining one's humanity (and often life itself) and accepting death as a human being (or perhaps physical death): whether one retained the freedom to choose autonomously one's attitude to extreme conditions even when they seemed totally beyond one's ability to influence them.

—Bruno Bettelheim, *The Informed Heart,* pp. 158–159

"SINGING your Song." This is psychological, not physical singing. It is based on . . . making inner accounts—that is, feeling what you are owed and recording it in memory. Everyone has a song to sing in this respect. If you really want to know what kinds of inner accounts you have made throughout your life, begin to notice the typical "songs you sing." . . . Sometimes people sing their songs without any encouragement and sometimes, after a few glasses of wine, they begin to sing openly. They sing about how badly they have been treated, about how they never had a real chance, about their past glories, about how they married wrongly, about how their parents did not understand them, about how nice they really are, about how they have been unappreciated, misunderstood, and so on, and all this means how everyone is to blame except themselves. All this is making *inner accounts,* or rather it is the result of making accounts. . . .

Why is it necessary to notice them, to starve them, to push them away, out of a central position in one's life, until they are sung only on rare occasions, in faint voice, and perhaps, finally, never? They cripple you inside. They take energy. You smile—bravely— you all know that brave smile—and it is all lies. A good singer . . . cannot get beyond himself. He is a victim of his own account-making. As soon as anything is difficult he begins singing. This stops him: he cannot grow. He perhaps begins to weep. He cannot change his level of being. He cannot get beyond what he *is*— i.e. crippled by sad songs. It is a sign of being. Being is what you *are* and to change being one must not be what one is. Instead of working on himself in some difficult situation, he begins to sing at once, perhaps very nicely and quietly. If he is criticized or spoken to sharply, he begins to pity himself, or gets furious, and feels he is not understood, and so on. And then he begins to sing, either softly to himself or to others, especially to people who will listen to him—or, it may be, to her. Often a person makes friends with another person only because it is easy to sing his or her song to him or her, and if the latter suddenly tells him in so many words to "shut up," he or she is so deeply offended that he goes in search of a new friend—a person who will really *understand* him or her, as the expression goes—as if anyone could understand another person, just like that. "If only," they say. To understand another, one must first understand oneself, and this only begins after long work on oneself and catching glimpses of what one is really like. A good singer certainly does not understand himself. He prefers to sing the song that he is misunderstood and so he dreams of a marvelous world in which everything is arranged so that he is the central figure in it. And this attitude and these dreams create a weakness and, in fact, a real, psychological sickness, for which a man may have to pay all through life.

　　　　　—Maurice Nicoll, *Psychological Commentaries,*
　　　　　　　　　　　　　　Vol. 1, pp. 254–255

WE MUST KNOW how to detach ourselves even from suffering. We must learn to be happy even when we are unhappy. We must, in a word, work loose from ourselves. A Father of the Church used to say to himself, "There is only one way of being cured of sadness, and that is to dislike being sad." It is hard to believe this when we are suffering. As if we had chosen to be hurt! Of course not, but what is terrible is that we often choose to keep on suffering, to fan the flames of our pain, to inflame our wounds, to find our only comfort in our very discomfort. For if we keep our pain, then we also keep our right to complain, our right to withdraw into our shell, our right to hurt others and to kill their joy. And when there is no joy in the world any longer, then we will be confirmed in our pain. We have, in the meantime, only one stone to rest our head on, and it is called despair. This hard pillow will give us long service.

　　　　　　　　　　　—Louis Evely, *Suffering,* p. 144

A GREAT REVERSAL of standpoint, calling for much sacrifice, is needed before we can see the world as "given" by the very nature of the psyche. It is so much more straightforward, more dramatic, impressive, and therefore more convincing, to see all the things that happen to me than to observe how I make them happen. Indeed, the animal nature of man makes him resist seeing himself as the maker of his circumstances.

　　　　—C. G. Jung, *Psychology and Religion: West and East,*
　　　　　　　　　　Vol. II in Collected Works, p. 514, par. 841

I HAD HEARD IT before, this thing of persons bringing on their own suffering and pain, but today I listened. Suddenly it had immediate relevance for me. Well, I suppose, not so suddenly, for it has been slowly coming for some time. But today it fully broke upon my consciousness.

It utterly astounds me to consider that I choose my pain. I'm sure that all pain cannot be explained this way, furthermore, it has always been so pleasing to think that my pain came from some organic problem, or the strains and stresses caused by other people and situations. But the evidence is quite clear. No one else lives my life for me, though often I try to squirm out of this truth. And how many times have I come to this same pain? I cannot remember.

I have attacked the pain countless times. But very infrequently have I dealt with the pattern of living that leads to the pain. In truth I like the pattern, but not the consequences. I sense something hopeful about this discovery, but I am more aware of being shattered.

—Roland R. Reece, "Notes from a Journal"

YOU MAY ASK: "What are these forms of suffering that we have to sacrifice?" There is the suffering of man towards woman, of woman towards man. For example, a man may feel that he has never met the woman who really understands him. Or he may feel simply that he has never been properly appreciated or given a chance, and so on. Or a woman may feel that she has never been married—or that she has never had any children—or that she is always having children—and this is her suffering. Then take all the mechanical forms of suffering that arise from feeling that you have never been understood by your parents, your husband, your wife, or your children. I think it would be impossible to enumerate all the forms of suffering that people form in themselves and cling to as the most valuable things in their lives. And it is exactly this suffering derived from life and all its awkwardness that has to be sacrificed. . . . Fraudulent suffering is the keynote to what we have to sacrifice. Real suffering is utterly different and always opens us to a higher level: fraudulent suffering closes us. It is extraordinary how a moment of real suffering makes everything false fall away from you.

. . . . .

You have heard that the only thing that we can sacrifice is our suffering. What does sacrifice mean? Sacrifice means originally *to make holy*. Does it mean that we have to make our suffering holy? No, its meaning is far deeper. As long as I identify with my suffering, as long as I ascribe it to myself, I will remain identified with it. Now whatever was made holy originally meant that with which all personal connection had been given up. It belonged then to God. If you like you can substitute for the word "holy" the word "conscious." You cannot become conscious of anything in yourself as long as you identify with it. To become really conscious of anything in yourself is to be no longer identified with it, no longer it. If I become conscious of my mechanical forms of suffering and internal account-making and my negative states, they are no longer me. I detach myself from them, I let them go, as it were, I no longer feel myself by means of them. As a result, my feeling of myself will change. This act allows transformation to work and whatever is real in your suffering you will meet on a higher level completely transformed into something else, but as long as you tie yourself down to your suffering and really feel yourself through your suffering—in fact, feel your own importance in this way—you cannot expect any transformation. As I once said long ago, it is like standing on a plank and trying to lift the plank. You have to step aside, and then it is quite easy to lift it.

—Maurice Nicoll, *Psychological Commentaries,*
Vol. 3, pp. 852, 897

THIS IS MAN'S GREAT and inalienable freedom—perhaps the only freedom he has—the freedom of his spirit to accept and be at one with life, or to revolt and be in separation. It is a fateful freedom, a tragic freedom if you will, but it is what gives dignity and purpose to the life of man. It is the power to cooperate with God in the work of creation and redemption—which cannot indeed be completed without man's cooperation.

. . . . .

Our task is to live fully and wisely "now," within the limits of our circumstances and of those relationships which are at once our joy and our sorrow, our opportunity and our restriction.

—E. Graham Howe and L. Le Mesurier, *The Open Way,* pp. 173–174, 180

ALL WHO HAVE REALLY suffered—in mind, body or estate—know that the hardest element in all suffering is not the actual pain (most people have a great deal of courage and dignity) but the apparent waste: the sense of futility, of emptiness, of uselessness. To be condemned to external inaction, to be confined within narrow limits, to be unable to use natural gifts, or to be denied some very human and natural outlet: in whatever form such trials may come, this is the aspect which embitters or depresses those who have to endure them. And it is this creative use of suffering as *action* and as *sacrifice* which transforms it. When we can offer ourselves to God so completely that the "dedicated life" of Christ is actually communicated to us—we are very near to God, the heart of reality. . . .

But for most people the "spiritual sacrifice" is made within—in heart and will—and is usually known to God alone. All that others see is a certain joy and serenity, a sureness in dealing with adverse conditions, which sometimes causes astonishment, but more often is taken for granted. The deep meaning of it all lies in the hidden personal life of worship and dedication.

—Olive Wyon, *The Altar Fire,* p. 74

EXERCISE 10

Consider voluntary suffering

We come now to a consideration of voluntary suffering—suffering that we are willing to take on in order that our own lives can be fully realized and in order that the world may be fully realized. But these are acts of creation, and creation involves risk—a painful dying to who we are now, a sacrifice of the known so that the unknown, uncertain new can come. This is why we do not change very often. Those who participate in change must participate in death, burial, and resurrection. "When Christ calls a man," wrote Bonhoeffer, "he bids him come and die." The apostles had so lived through the experience of Easter that they not only wanted to take its message to the world, but went rejoicing that "they were counted worthy to suffer dishonor for the name."

This week, consider first what is a goal for your own life that you are willing to suffer to attain. Try to be specific about what you are willing to bear in your own becoming. Are you willing to suffer insecurity? Are you willing to take upon yourself the burden of anxiety? Are you willing to suffer being cut off from the close community of people whose esteem and friendship you value? Are you willing to suffer the possibility of being poor? All these some have suffered in order that change might come to the hardened structures within themselves.

Second, consider what you are willing to endure so that change can come to the hardened dehumanizing structures in the world that shape the lives of people. If you find a self that does not really care very much about the misery of others, or has a lot of personal matters to attend to first, allow it to make confession. It may belong to a time of crippling physical or emotional poverty in your life. Pray for its healing. Its wounds now make it turn from the need of others, but it can reach another understanding and be shown another way.

BELOVED, DO NOT be surprised at the fiery ordeal which comes upon you to prove you, as though something strange were happening to you. But rejoice in so far as you share Christ's sufferings, that you may also rejoice and be glad when his glory is revealed. If you are reproached for the name of Christ, you are blessed, because the spirit of glory and of God rests upon you. But let none of you suffer as a murderer, or a thief, or a wrongdoer, or a mischief-maker; yet if one suffers as a Christian, let him not be ashamed, but under that name let him glorify God. For the time has come for judgment to begin with the household of God; and if it begins with us, what will be the end of those who do not obey the gospel of God? And

"If the righteous man is scarcely saved,
where will the impious and sinner appear?"

Therefore, let those who suffer according to God's will do right and entrust their souls to a faithful creator.

—1 Peter 4:12–19 (RSV)

WHILE ALL MEN ARE thus religious, by no means are all forms of religion equally creative or uncreative. The common idea that a man's religion is a purely subjective and personal matter, without relevance to his behavior or character is, I believe, quite false. It separates inward commitment and outward behavior, which are intimately related. It is, in fact, the otherwise admirable trait of loyalty to one's family, one's group or nation, which when it becomes central, is the root of much of the injustice, pride, and selfishness we have described and with which we are surrounded.

The only hope in the human situation is that the "religiousness" of men find its true center in God, and not in the many idols that appear in the course of our experience. If men are to forget themselves enough to share with each other, to be honest under pressure, and to be rational and moral enough to establish community, they must have some center of loyalty and devotion, some source of security and meaning, beyond their own welfare.

This center of loyalty beyond themselves cannot be a human

creation, greater than the individual but still finite, such as the family, the nation, tradition, race, or the church. Only the God who created all men and so represents none of them exclusively; only the God who rules all history and so is the instrument of no particular historical movement; only the God who judges His faithful as well as their enemies, and loves and cares for all, can be the creative center of human existence.

The ultimate concern of each man must raise him above his struggles with his neighbor instead of making these conflicts more bitter and intense. Given an ultimate security in God's eternal love, and an ultimate meaning to his own small life in God's eternal purposes, a man can forget his own welfare and for the first time look at his neighbor free from the gnawings of self-concern.

．　．　．　．　．

After a day of such heated discussions, I came back to my room struck with the intense difficulty that each of us has in being truly humane to our fellows, and the infinitely subtle ways in which we are able to avoid facing up to this difficulty. The pressures of self-interest in this case were, of course, immense. This was especially true in the case of those men and women responsible for hungry children.

When one is hungry, and when the threat of worse hunger to come nags continually at the subconscious, then even seven and one-half immense parcels hardly seem enough. We begin to picture to ourselves the dread time when even those seven will be gone. So the prospect of losing any one of them to our neighbors—of having only three or four instead of six or seven—creates as much anxiety of spirit as had been there before the parcels came.

In the possession of material goods, there is no such thing as satiety. One seems never able to accumulate enough to be a safe-guard against the unpredictable future, and so the requirements of full security remain in principle unlimited. Thus, men who otherwise appeared quite normal and respectable were goaded by their insistent fears about the future into claiming all they could for themselves and their own. And concurrently, the needs of the neighbor receded into the dim background. Men in such a situation seemed hardly free to do the generous thing, but only free enough to act in their own self-interest.

As Brecht puts it in the *Threepenny Opera:*

> For even saintly folk will act like sinners
> Unless they have their customary dinners.

> —Langdon Gilkey, *Shantung Compound,*
> pp. 233–234, 111

In the introduction to this unit I said that in the mission groups of my church we had each written our autobiography to reflect on how suffering had shaped our lives for ministry. The following is an excerpt from the story of Gordon Cosby which he wrote as part of the group procedure:

Then came Pearl Harbor and our country's involvement in World War II. Nothing in my background had prepared me to critically examine our nation's call to arms. Although I volunteered and did an effective job of spiritual nurture for the men, two and a half years later I knew that I had participated in my last war and would never again encourage another to be a good soldier. I can respect another's commitment to the country's armed forces but never again would I be able to help with the morale building. Now there was a new connection between trusting Christ's redeeming love for us in his cross for my eternal salvation and the application of that love toward my country and my country's enemies. I might well need to die for them; I could never help to kill them.

Yet, those two and a half war years during which I served as a spiritual guide to three thousand exceptional men shaped the course of my life. All the men had volunteered for airborne service as paratroopers and glider men. Most of them had volunteered because of an exceptional spirit of adventure or because they had gotten in trouble and had been given the option of volunteering in the airborne in lieu of serving time in the guardhouse. There were not many conventionally religious men among them. In the

presence of such men, who hourly faced death and dying, that which
is inauthentic in one's faith is quickly detected and exposed. Picture
thousands of men scattered over scores of miles under enemy fire
for weeks at a time. Imagine the impossibility of their gathering
in substantial numbers in any one location. Imagine the difficulty
of being with any substantial number of them, even if one spent
his days and nights making pastoral calls in their foxholes. How to
reach these men at a time when they more desperately needed to
hear Gospel and be nurtured in the faith than ever before in their
lives? Out of sheer necessity I identified the pastoral gift of one or
two men in each of the twelve companies in my regiment. Here,
then, was born the idea and the practice of small nurturing mission
groups. Thus, each of the three thousand men had access to the
witness and nurture of Christians, if they so desired. This experience was translated into a civilian situation when the Church of the
Saviour came into being in 1947.

There are great differences but some similarities between the experience of men in the army under combat conditions and the
prison experience of men like Bonhoeffer and Father Delp. All of
surrounding society is in chaos. None of the traditional values hold
because they are traditional. You are constantly in the presence of
elemental human suffering in its agonizing extremes. Much of the
time you are in the immediate presence of death. You live with
the reality and the stench of it. And you often have time to reflect.
In winter, the nights are long—and there are countless hours of
waiting. This is a rare combination for being driven into the deeps
of one's soul and into the arms of God and the peace which the
world has never given.

Brother Lawrence saw the bare branches of a tree in winter;
Amos a plumb line, and Jeremiah an almond tree. Perhaps it makes
no difference what one sees. I saw a face—a beloved bloated, dis-
colored dead face. I had spent the day lifting, loading and un-
loading bodies. Then they all were in a field, designated a new
cemetery. How many? Five hundred, perhaps a thousand! Mounds
of death! What difference how many! Then I went with my alco-

holic friend and jeep driver to a lonely field some miles away. Here I was to bury my dearest friend—a friend in Christ; a friend who shared a vision of what was then dimly seen, but who had intended to help me bring it to fruition. Though there was no name then by which to call it, we had talked together many hours about the Church of the Saviour. Now this magnificent specimen of manhood was dead. His body was decomposing. The cold June rain was falling. Powerfully disciplined German panzer troops were a few miles away covering the Normandy countryside. With a damp New Testament in my hand opened at I Corinthians 15, save for one spared wizened alcoholic at my side, I was alone with an impossible dream. I knew the power of envy, a strange envy. The envy of my friend who was experiencing that which was denied to me for a while. I knew the power of the resurrection in the midst of unbearable loneliness and death. From that moment I knew that I could go on alone if necessary. Faithfulness to what I had seen did not depend upon human support. Those agonizing years were to make me singularly unconcerned with "success." Also I felt delivered in large measure from the fear of death. I was to be close to it many times during the next months, but its sting had been removed. The impact of this quality of experiencing is difficult to describe. It is so vivid and real that afterwards it is as hard to disbelieve as before it was hard to believe. There is another realm! To touch it is to live. To become immersed in it is the only worthwhile pursuit, to give it to others the deepest joy.

—N. Gordon Cosby, Minister, Church of the Saviour

NEITHER PASTOR NOR his counselee, therefore, can effectively and enduringly resolve anxiety apart from the redemptive fellowship of the Christian community. One central quality has characterized all kinds of anxiety as described in this book: *loneliness*. Economic anxiety tends to isolate men from each other; the feeling of creaturely finitude makes of mankind a "lonely crowd," to use Reisman's phrase. The grief-stricken person is likely to feel as did the Ancient Mariner: "Alone, alone, all, all alone; alone on a wide, wide sea."

The sin-sick soul feels that no one could possibly understand him in his evil condition. The person suffering from the anxiety of legalism feels that he must earn his salvation singlehanded. The morally indifferent are not even aware of the need for relatedness, and how great is their unrelatedness!

As all these anxieties coalesce in the necessity of a death, burial, and resurrection, and as the individual moves into salvation "with fear and trembling," even then the anxiety of the cross and the experience of holy dread become most acute when the individual realizes that he is "alone before God." He would fain shrink back, but the act of faith calls for his staying with the struggle of the soul without an "umpire" between him and God.

But when a person moves through the depths of the experience of anxiety in the creative directions that are implicit in the intention of God for man's security, a real reversal takes place. The shrinking lonely ones turn and seek community with those who will understand from experience the real change that has taken place. The result of this movement of persons who have partaken of the sufferings of Jesus Christ is a fellowship of suffering and a fellowship of concern. The participants bear one another's burden and so fulfill the law of Christ. Those who have been comforted of God become a comfort to those who are in any affliction by means of the comfort with which they themselves have been comforted of God.

—Wayne E. Oates, *Anxiety in Christian Experience,* pp. 152–153

HENCE man's liberation from social forms which oppress and enslave him has an enormous moral and religious significance and puts before him the moral and religious problem in its pure form. Man's liberation from social oppression shows that the pain and suffering of life is not due to social causes and cannot be cured by them. Herein lies the paradox of the relations between the individual and society. Life becomes outwardly less tragic as a result of liberation from social fetters and prejudices, but inwardly its eternally tragic nature is deepened and intensified. Man's social liberation shows how false, superficial and illusory are all social dreams and utopias. This does not mean of course that one must not struggle for social liberation. One must struggle for it if only in order to reveal the depths of life and its inner conflicts; liberation thus acquires a spiritual, religious and moral significance. Thus the object of freeing love from social fetters, prejudices and restrictions is not to enable people to enjoy love and satisfy their desires, but to reveal love's inner tragedy, depth and earnestness. It is the same in everything. It is true of all freedom. For freedom is not satisfaction, delight and ease, but pain, toil and difficulty. A time must come in the life of man when he will take upon himself the burden of freedom, for he will come spiritually of age. In freedom life will be harder, more tragic and fuller of responsibility. The ethics of freedom is stern and demands heroism.

—Nicolas Berdyaev, *The Destiny of Man,* p. 158

NOW, WHEN A MAN consents to live and die for the truth, he sets in motion spiritual rhythms whose outward influences are, in the nature of things, simply immeasurable. I take the courts as one symbol of Gandhi's method. What indeed did he hope for, from that vantage point? He hoped to say to others something that had come to have the deepest meaning for himself. Out of a virile disregard for personal danger and stress, he wished to make it possible for others to live—to be conscious, to be freed of demons, to welcome their brothers. The point, I would think, for Gandhi and Jesus, is not that men would agree with them, or do the same things they did. The point is that others would come to a deepened consciousness; that their sense of existence and human issues would be sharpened to the point where they would "do their thing"—a good thing, a human thing, as they were doing theirs.

. . . . .

We have assumed the name of peacemakers, but we have been, by and large, unwilling to pay any significant price. And because we want the peace with half a heart and half a life and will, the war, of course, continues, because the waging of war, by its nature, is total—but the waging of peace, by our own cowardice, is partial. So a whole will and a whole heart and a whole national life bent toward war prevail over the velleities of peace. In every national war since the founding of the republic we have taken for granted that war shall exact the most rigorous cost, and that the cost shall be paid with a cheerful heart. We take it for granted that in wartime families will be separated for long periods, that men will be imprisoned, wounded, driven insane, killed on foreign shores. In favor of such wars, we declare a moratorium on every normal human hope—for marriage, for community, for friendship, for moral conduct toward strangers and the innocent. We are instructed that deprivation and discipline, private grief and public obedience are to be our lot. And we obey. And we bear with it—because bear we must—because war is war, and good war or bad, we are stuck with it and its cost.

But what of the price of peace? I think of the good, decent, peace-loving people I have known by the thousands, and I wonder. How many of them are so afflicted with the wasting disease of normalcy that, even as they declare for the peace, their hands reach out with an instinctive spasm in the direction of their loved ones, in the direction of their comforts, their home, their security, their income, their future, their plans—that five-year plan of studies, that ten-year plan of professional status, that twenty-year plan of family growth and unity, that fifty-year plan of decent life and honorable natural demise. "Of course, let us have the peace," we cry, "but at the same time let us have normalcy, let us lose nothing, let our lives stand intact, let us know neither prison nor ill repute nor disruption of ties." And because we must encompass this and protect that, and because at all costs—at all costs—our hopes must march on schedule, and because it is unheard of that in the name of peace a sword should fall, disjoining that fine and cunning web that our lives have woven, because it is unheard of that good men should suffer injustice or families be sundered or good repute be lost—because of this we cry peace and cry peace, and there is no peace. There is no peace because there are no peacemakers. There are no makers of peace because the making of peace is at least as costly as the making of war—at least as exigent, at least as disruptive, at least as liable to bring disgrace and prison and death in its wake.

.   .   .   .   .

A gathering was held within the last year in Mexico, consisting of some twenty persons from the peace communities of North America. The question arose at a certain point: "What makes a man peaceable?" The question had been intensely discussed for some time, with one of the participants remaining silent. Finally, when he was pressed as to his thought, he remarked simply, "I believe there is enough latent violence in this room to begin a war."

A long and somewhat shocked silence followed. Could it be true, each one was thinking, that in his heart, which he had fancied was the heart of a peacemaker, there lay the unexorcised will to murder? The thought was disturbing and portentous.

The silence then was broken by a second question addressed to the same speaker. "If this is indeed true, then what is required in order to stop a war?"

And the same silent man spoke again, in his direct and simple fashion. "You know, I think that someone would be required to die."

—Daniel Berrigan, *No Bars to Manhood,* pp. 56, 57–58, 71

"THE LEVEL OF BEING of a man attracts his life." This saying applies to humanity in general—that is, the general level of humanity with regard to its being attracts the form of life that it experiences. It is useless to think that wars and horrors and revolutions, etc., are exceptional. What is at fault is the level of being of people. But nobody is willing to understand this and whenever war takes place, as I said, people take it as exceptional, and even speak about a future free from war, as soon as the existing war is over. We can see the same process at work now. History repeats itself because man remains at the same level of being—namely, he attracts again and again the same circumstances, feels the same things, says the same

things, hopes the same things, believes the same things. And yet nothing actually changes. All the articles that were written in the last war are just the same as the articles written in this war, and will be for ever and ever. But what concerns us more is that the same idea applies to ourselves, to each individual person. As long as there is no change in the level of being, the personal history of a man remains the same. Everything repeats itself in his own life: he says the same things, he does the same things, he regrets the same things, he commits the same things. And all this belongs to this immensely deep idea that the level of being attracts his life.
—Maurice Nicoll, *Psychological Commentaries,* Vol. 1, pp. 1–2

THE belief in the redemption of evil does not mean any security of salvation. The prophets of Israel, writes Buber, "always aimed to shatter all security and to proclaim in the opened abyss of the final insecurity the unwished-for God who demands that His human creatures become real . . . and confounds all who imagine that they can take refuge in the certainty that the temple of God is in their midst." There is no other path for the responsible modern man than this "holy insecurity." In an age in which "God is dead," the truly religious man sets forth across the God-deprived reality to a new meeting with the nameless God and on his way destroys the images that no longer do justice to God. "Holy insecurity" is life lived in the Face of God. It is the life in which one learns to speak the truth "no matter whether a whole people is listening, or only a few individuals," and learns to speak it quietly and clearly through having been in hell and having returned to the light of day again.

If a man tries to get rid of his insecurity by constructing a defensive armour to protect himself from the world, he has added to the exposedness which is the state of all men the hysteria which makes him run blindly from the thing he fears rather than face and accept it. Conversely, if he accepts his exposed condition and remains open to those things which meet him, he has turned his exposedness into "holy insecurity." He has overcome his blind fear

and has put in its place the faith which is born out of the relation
with the Thou. The defensive man becomes literally rigid with
fear. He sets between himself and the world a rigid religious dogma,
a rigid system of philosophy, a rigid political belief and commitment to a group, and a rigid wall of personal values and habits.
The open man, on the other hand, accepts his fear and relaxes into
it. He substitutes the realism of despair, if need be, for the tension
of hysteria. He meets every new situation with quiet and sureness out
of the depths of his being, yet he meets it with the fear and trembling of one who has no ready-made answer to life.

—Maurice S. Friedman, *Martin Buber: The Life of Dialogue,*
pp. 135–136

THE GREATEST MYSTERY of life is that satisfaction is felt not by those
who take and make demands but by those who give and make
sacrifices. In them alone the energy of life does not fail, and this
is precisely what is meant by creativeness. Therefore the positive
mystery of life is to be found in love, in sacrificial, giving, creative
love. As has been said already, all creativeness is love and all love
is creative. If you want to receive, give, if you want to obtain satisfaction, do not seek it, never think of it and forget the very word;
if you want to acquire strength, manifest it, give it to others. . . .

—Nicolas Berdyaev, *The Destiny of Man,* p. 141

AS THE SELF GROWS and emerges from this primordial self-related-
ness a new aspect of self-giving appears. For the self can grow only
by overcoming fixation at any point in its becoming. The self seeks
integrity; but there can be no integrity without change. This is the
hard lesson. It means that in every becoming there is some surrender of present satisfactions, defenses and securities to a new
demand. The past is not rejected. It remains a dynamic part of the
personality, even when lost from conscious memory. But no past is
sufficient for the new present, and no past form of the self's being
can be preserved unaltered. This may seem a commonplace, yet it
is the source of the desperate battle of the self for life, and it is

here that tempation enters. Change means risk, and risk is painful.
We are willing to grow provided we know we can maintain or increase our present security, but this can never be absolutely known.
We begin to "save our life" by holding on to it as it is. It is the
first manifestation of the Fall.

The objective self at a given moment is largely the deposit of
experience as shaped by our self-understanding. This given self
bears its freight of hurt and hope, its creativity and anxiety, its
self-seeking, and its groping for love. We cling to this self as it is.
We fear it is all we have. Even its sufferings are familiar and we
clutch them because their very familiarity is comforting, and saves us
from facing the deeper suffering hidden underneath. We usually
would rather live with our present frustrations than risk acquiring
new ones. Yet so long as we aim at the maintenance of this present
self, as we now conceive it, we cannot enter the larger selfhood
which is pressing for life. This natural resistance of the self to becoming is not in itself sin. It is a self-protective device of the human
spirit; but when it becomes an invitation to use our freedom against
the risk of becoming it is temptation to sin. The meaning of sin is
usually not that we try to make ourselves the centre of everything.
That may happen, but it is a monstrous perversion. We are usually
more subtle. We make our present state of selfhood the meaning of
existence, and thus refuse the deeper meaning which lies within
and beyond this present. When that refusal becomes refusal to trust
in the giver of life and the greater community he is creating it is
sin. . . .

.   .   .   .   .

Whatever opens the person to the richness of the world beyond
himself, whatever encourages the mind to give itself to the search
for what is there to be known, whatever releases the person from
defensiveness about his present structure of thought, and whatever
overcomes distraction and triviality in the search for truth, contributes to the work of reason. And here surely we are not far
from a definition of love. It will be recalled that the categorical
analysis of love stresses the freedom to enter into relation with the

other, and to set the other free to be himself. Love means willingness to participate in the being of the other at the cost of suffering
and with the expectation of mutual enrichment, criticism and
growth. Love gives to the search for knowledge the indispensable
personal context and spirit in which reason can work successfully
and bring knowledge into the service of the fulfillment of personal
being. Reason needs the spirit and impetus of love to realize itself
and to become the servant of the Kingdom of God.

Whatever gives the person a motive for searching, for continuing
the struggle for knowledge, for enduring the pain of creativity in
the realm of ideas will be of service to reason.

.   .   .   .

But man seeks community with the source of his being. It is the
God relationship which makes a man a man. Man is linked with the
whole of things, with eternity and time, with the open future as
well as the past, with the source and end of his being as well as with
his most intensely satisfying present loves. The self craves the
completely trustworthy fulfillment of the will to belong. Only to
whatever fulfills our being can we give ourselves without despair.

The Christian Gospel asserts the reality of such an absolute in
the Kingdom of God. We are created to find ourselves in belonging, and we really belong to that which makes us lovers. The only
commitment which can sustain an absolute trust is that which
accepts what we are in all the conditions of finitude, and yet offers
participation in the infinitely creative life which takes our present
loves beyond themselves into the service of God. It is the trivial
faiths and pseudo-religions which offer satisfaction to the self as it
is, or as it ideally projects its wishes. The truth in the Gospel which
cuts into all our loves is that every love must be offered up to the
creative transformation which God is bringing about in the whole
creation.

—Daniel Day Williams, *The Spirit and the Forms of Love,*
pp. 206, 287, 209

ACCEPTANCE OF A SHARE, still more the willing acceptance of more than our full share, in the tragedy of life—a tragedy in which God, as well as man, is an actor—is positive; it has about it something vitalizing. . . . Those who meet pain clear-eyed, and with a positive and active acceptance, who "face the music" as the slang phrase has it; those who are not only ready to do their bit, but to share their bit in the world's sorrow, make a great discovery. They find not only that they are enabled to bear their sorrow in a way which hurts less—for that which hurts most in the bearing is that which is most resented; what is most freely accepted hurts least—but that they achieve an enrichment and a growth in personality which makes them centers of influence and light in ways of which they never suspected the possibility. Few things can so inspire and re-create the human heart as the spectacle of crushing misfortune cheerfully and heroically borne; and the unconscious influence which those exert is far greater than they or others comprehend. Suffering lightly borne is constructive work . . . for pain conquered is power.

—Lily Dougall, *God's Way and Man*

TO BE A FATHER is precisely to suffer; to become a father is to become vulnerable. As long as one is young, one is hard, selfish, protected. No doubt, one has terrible blues, emotions, melancholies, but one holds one's own pretty well, one withdraws easily, one suffers only for oneself. Our compassion for others is gratuitous, generous, superfluous. But when one becomes a father, or a mother, one suddenly sees oneself as vulnerable, in the most sensitive part of one's being; one is completely powerless to defend oneself, one is no longer free, one is tied up. To become a father is to experience an infinite dependency on an infinitely small, frail being, dependent on us and therefore omnipotent over our heart. Oh, we really depend on people who depend on us! The strong person who loves a weak person has put his happiness at his mercy. He depends on him henceforth. He is without any defense against him. To love a person is inevitably to depend on him, to give him power over us. God loved us freely, God gave us power over him. God wanted to have need of us. The passion is the revelation of our terrible power over God. He surrendered himself to us, we had him at our disposal, we did with him what we wanted. On a plaque in Normandy one can read this cruel sentence: "It is always the one who loves the least who is the strongest."

—Louis Evely, *Suffering*, p. 126

IT IS THE TOLERANCE of the orthodox which best shows how completely Christianity is lost. Their solution is: if only we may keep our faith for ourselves, the world can take care of itself. Merciful God, and that is supposed to be Christianity. That is the power which once broke upon the world and through readiness to suffer forced Christianity on the world, compelled it more forcefully than any tyrant.

The orthodox do not even suspect that this, their tolerance, is the effect of sheer worldliness, because they have not really either understanding, respect or courage for martyrdom or a true belief in eternity, but really desire to have a good time in this world. . . .

How low has Christianity sunk, how powerless and miserable it has become! It is reason that has conquered: reason that has tyrannized enthusiasm and the like, making it ridiculous. That is why people dare not be enthusiastic, . . . they are afraid of being laughed at instead of put to death.

—Søren Kierkegaard, *Journals*, (1849), p. 126

IF, HOWEVER, God is born as a man and wants to unite mankind in the fellowship of the Holy Ghost, he must suffer the terrible torture of having to endure the world in all its reality. This is the cross he has to bear, and he himself is a cross. The whole world is God's suffering, and every individual man who wants to get anywhere near his own wholeness knows that this is the way of the cross.

—C. G. Jung, *Psychology and Religion: West and East,*
Vol. II in Collected Works, p. 179, par. 265

WHAT USE ARE all the lessons learned through our suffering and misery if no bridge can be thrown from our side to the other shore?

What is the point of our revulsion from error and fear if it brings
no enlightenment, does not penetrate the darkness and dispel it?
What use is it shuddering at the world's coldness, which all the
time grows more intense, if we cannot discover the grace to conjure
up visions of better conditions?

—Alfred Delp, S.J., *The Prison Meditations of Father Delp,*
pp. 20–21

EUNICE

"How did I feel?
I felt all throwed away
Like an old shoe in the rain
Or a chicken heart
In a butcher's hand
Was how I felt,
And blue as a week of Mondays."

"I felt," she said,
"Shades blacker than my skin,
 Like there wasn't no place
 Low enough
 To hide my feelings in."

"It wasn't," she said,
"The jail I was in
 But the world I was out of
 Made me cry.
 Not that I was so wrong,
 But nobody else was right
 Is why."

"You don't know
 What a bad time is.
 Girl, you livin' child's play

Til they sweep you under the rug
And you feel
All throwed away."
—Sheila Alexander, *Minnesota Review,* Summer, 1961

DOES A DAY GO BY when I do not think, "Lord, let this cup pass
from me?" Does a day go by when I do not look at those who pass
me on the street and envy them their problems and their lives? I
did not choose to immerse my being in the revolutionary process. I
was chosen and I was told that the only reward was knowing that I
was a part of the revolutionary process. I, too, am afraid, I wrote
her. Afraid that one time when I am tested, I will fail. Afraid that
one time when I need strength, I will not have the will to bring it
into being. Sometimes it hurts so much and I am just one person
and one person can't stop the world from crying. God, how I hate
them! I want to live, too! I don't want to fight a revolution. I
want to be happy and enjoy my children and sit in the park with
Joan and write lyric poetry. God, if only they would stop hurting
people, we wouldn't have to relinquish our claims to our lives. But
the sun shines on the running sores of humanity and all else is
irrelevant.

.   .   .   .   .

When I finished her letter, I knew that she would be with us as
we started the ascent toward the plateau where we built our next
camp. I was sorry she didn't understand why a black man could not
care that she, too, was a woman, but one day she would. We are
victims, all of us now making our way through the wilderness. We
were victims before we were born and sometimes our hatred of
what was done to us threatens to destroy all that we want to be, all
that we can be. If we hate the past more than we love the future,
we will succeed in bringing that past into the future and those who
come afterward will find our bones on the desert sand.

I, too, am afraid, I wrote her, afraid that not only will I not make
it to the Promised Land, but that I will forget the vision I saw from
the mountaintop. And if we forget the vision, we have lost, no

matter how many thousands walk with us. But how hard it is, my God how hard it is, to keep the vision when everyone's pain has become your own. O God God God why can't I hate them?

I can, but I mustn't.

We are not what we know we can be, but we must not let despair immobilize us. More than anything, perhaps, the revolutionary needs faith, the faith of the Old Testament prophets, the faith of Meister Eckhart and the desert mystics, because it is only faith which will sustain us when the first excitement dies. Faith is a necessary prerequisite for commitment. It is not a blind faith, however, but a faith rooted in the knowledge that the revolution proceeds, not in an unbroken ascent, but by fits and starts. It is a faith which allows us to remove ourselves enough from events to look at them and see that what feels bad may, in essence, be good and what exhilarates us may be detrimental to the journey on which we have started. Faith will not keep us from making mistakes. It will sustain us, however, when the mistakes are inevitably made.

There is no human endeavor more difficult than the search for the New Land. Well, we shall try. We may not succeed, but we must do what we can.

Our humanity demands it of us.

— Julius Lester, *Search for the New Land,* pp. 192, 194

[JOHN] WOOLMAN'S SENSITIVITY to suffering included not only the various members of the human race, but all of God's creatures. This sensitivity caused him, on his English journey, to do something that seemed, to many, singular or even quixotic. Noting that the stage coaches were able to keep to their schedules over bad roads only by overworking the horses, he decided to walk from London to York. By the route that he chose, this walking journey was of at least 400 miles. He was also influenced by the suffering of the boys who were employed in handling horses and coaches. "Stage Coaches," he reported, "frequently go upwards of a hundred miles in 24 hours, and I have heard friends say, in several places, that it is common for horses to be killed with hard driving, and many others are driven till they go blind." The tender man was well aware that he was personally unable to stop a practice that troubled him, but he also knew that he could at least refuse to profit by it. Not only did Woolman refuse to ride; he also refused to make use of the coaches in sending letters even cautioning friends not to send letters to him "on any common occasion by post."

The probability is that Woolman's self-denial, arising out of his deep sensitivity to the suffering of his fellow creatures, hastened his own death. When he was stricken with smallpox in York, he was well attended by his English hosts, but the journey had weakened him and the man often mentioned as the one authentic American saint died at the too early age of fifty-two. He died, as he lived, in the effort to watch diligently against "the motions of self" in his own mind. . . .

—Elton Trueblood, *The New Man for Our Time,* p. 54

AS THE FATHER has loved me, so have I loved you; abide in my love. If you keep my commandments; you will abide in my love, just as I have kept my Father's commandments and abide in his love. These things I have spoken to you, that my joy may be in you, and that your joy may be full.

This is my commandment, that you love one another as I have loved you. Greater love has no man than this, that a man lay down his life for his friends.

—John 15: 9–13 (RSV)

I AM THE GOOD SHEPHERD: I know my own and my own know me, as the Father knows me and I know the Father; and I lay down my life for the sheep. And I have other sheep, that are not of this fold; I must bring them also, and they will heed my voice. So there shall be one flock, one shepherd. For this reason the Father loves me, because I lay down my life, that I may take it again. No one takes it from me, but I lay it down of my own accord. I have power to lay it down, and I have power to take it again; this charge I have received from my Father.

—John 10: 14–18 (RSV)

EXERCISE 11

Write your autobiography

Do you know what it means to be chosen? Have you ever thought of yourself as chosen? If you did believe this—if you could overcome all your resistances to the idea—would you live your life differently? What would it do to your concept of yourself? Would you act with more pride or more humility?

Reflecting on your whole life, can you see God acting, preparing you for ministry in this present hour? Write a two- or three-page paper including your response to the above question. Note especially the sufferings that crippled you for ministry and those that enabled you to take your place in the tradition of the suffering servant. "With His stripes we are healed." This is also true for His disciples. Celebration and suffering, to our surprise, are closely related. If we are not acquainted with our own suffering, others will instinctively know it. Our wounds do not even have to be healed. We simply have to be conscious of them. If we have not been wounded, we do not know what it feels like. We cannot say to another, "I understand."

It is not out of our perfection that we heal, but out of our acquaintance with pain.

Use for meditation the story of Joseph and his brothers and the material which follows from the lives of three extraordinary men.

AND NOW HAPPENED one of those curious coincidences which the
tangled skein of the war sometimes provided. Captain Payne Best,
one of the two British officers taken prisoner on the borders of
Holland in 1940 by means of a German hoax, who had been a
prisoner in Sachsenhausen during the last year, was transferred to
Buchenwald two weeks after Bonhoeffer's arrival and shared in his
adventures during the last weeks of his life. This detached and
ironical spectator, highly trained in the arts of critical observation,
and without any knowledge of Bonhoeffer's previous history, appreciated without reserve the spiritual stature to which he had now
attained. "Bonhoeffer," he wrote, "was different; just quite calm and
normal, seemingly perfectly at his ease . . . his soul really shone in
the dark desperation of our prison."

Bonhoeffer was passing the last landmarks in his spiritual journey. The struggles of the Tegel days had ended in victory, and he
seems to have attained that peace which is the gift of God and not
as the world giveth. The struggle to abandon to God his rich and
treasured past, the struggle with the last vestiges of his pride, the
struggle to suffer, in full measure and yet in gratitude, his human
longings and to remain open to others in the midst of his own pain;
all this had led him to that experience of the Cross, in which at last,
through a grasp of reality so intense that it fused all the elements of
his being into a single shining whole, he learnt what life can be
when "we throw ourselves completely into the arms of God, taking
seriously not our own sufferings, but the sufferings of God in the
world." Out of this death to the last vestiges of self Bonhoeffer
seems to have been raised up quietly, unspectacularly, into the last
stage of his life, in which he was made whole, made single, finally
integrated in Christ. In a way more complete than any that had gone
before, the Christian had become "the man for others," the disciple
"as his Lord."

As we look back, struggling with such help as we have to pierce
the obscurity that surrounds him in these last months, this seems to
be the truth. To claim it is to claim a definite event, a concrete happening, not sudden in the sense of being discontinuous with what

had gone before, but actual in the sense that it represents an inten-
sive experience of spiritual reality, a condition of being united to
God to an extent unknown until it is known from within, and which
saints throughout all the Christian centuries have struggled in vain
to describe. Apart from the change discernible in his letters after
July 21st, 1944, Bonhoeffer himself has left no record of it, and it
seems unlikely that he himself was conscious of it as of the consum-
mating stage in his spiritual development, although in his Tegel
days he had once written: "If I were to end my life here, in these
conditions, that would have a meaning that I think I could understand."

Those looking back to that life and striving to discover, here and
there, traces of that meaning which unfolds at a deeper level than
the exterior event, have no right to do more than touch it lightly,
and with the reserve that Bonhoeffer, in a like situation, would have
imposed upon himself. The most it would be fair to say is that there
are one or two indications of a profound and subtle change, and
that the man who could, for instance, write in 1944: "I have had
to take a new line with the companion of my daily walks . . . a
remark he let fall . . . has made me more offhanded and cool to
him than I have ever been to anyone before . . . I have even seen
to it that he has been deprived of certain little comforts. . . ." was
hardly the man of whom Payne Best could write: "Bonhoeffer was
all humility and sweetness." It is the "all" which seems the opera-
tive word here, and the passage continues: "He always seemed to
diffuse an atmosphere of happiness, of joy in every smallest event in
life, and of deep gratitude for the mere fact that he was alive," and
at the end of this sober, factual passage, Best quietly exposes the
roots of the matter, "He was one of the very few men I have ever
met to whom his God was real, and ever close to him."

And meanwhile though hopes and fears still alternated for Bonhoeffer, as for others, amid the continual uncertainties of these last
phantasmagoric days, fear in the deeper areas of his being was gone.
"He had always been afraid," Best wrote later to Sabine Leibholz,

"that he would not be strong enough to stand such a test, but now he knew that there was nothing in life of which one need ever be afraid. . . ."

Tragically, in the very last weeks of the war, the diary of Admiral Canaris had been found, full of damning material. Upon this Saturday which Bonhoeffer was passing at Schönberg surrounded by his hopeful companions, Huppenkothen, his one-time interrogator in Berlin, arrived at Flossenburg with orders for the immediate summary trial and execution of Canaris, Sack, Oster, two others of whom one was Müller's friend Gehre, and finally Dietrich Bonhoeffer. During the night of Saturday, search was made for Bonhoeffer through the cells in the camp. Von Schlabrendorff, who was one of the inmates, was twice woken and accused of being the wanted prisoner. At last the search was given up. Bonhoeffer must have travelled on southwards with the transport from Buchenwald. Well, mistakes could still be rectified. Petrol and a prison van were provided. In the morning of April 8th, the transport set out for Schönberg.

Meanwhile, in the schoolhouse at Schönberg, Low Sunday had dawned. It occurred to Pünder to ask Bonhoeffer to hold a small service. Bonhoeffer hesitated; most of his companions were Roman Catholic, and there was Kokorin from Communist Russia. But Kokorin himself begged for it, and under general pressure Bonhoeffer yielded. He gave an exposition of the Scripture passages for the day: "Through his stripes we are healed" (Isaiah 53:5) and "Blessed be the God and Father of our Lord Jesus Christ, which according to his abundant mercy hath begotten us again into a lively hope by the resurrection of Jesus Christ from the dead" (I Peter 1:3). "He reached the hearts of all," Payne Best remembers, "finding just the right words to express the spirit of our imprisonment, and the thoughts and resolutions which it had brought." Together with Bonhoeffer, all looked forward thankfully and hopefully into the future. The little service ended. Then, during the moment of stillness that succeeded it, the door was flung open and two men stood in the doorway. "Prisoner Bonhoeffer, take your things and come with us."

Bonhoeffer gathered his few belongings. In a copy of Plutarch that he had received for his birthday he wrote his name in large letters and left it on the table. His last words to Payne Best were a message to his trusted English friend Bishop Bell. "Tell him," he said, "that for me this is the end, but also the beginning. With him I believe in the principle of our universal Christian brotherhood which rises above all national interests, and that our victory is certain— Tell him too that I have never forgotten his words at our last meeting."

It must have been evening before Bonhoeffer reached Flossenburg. The "trial" went on throughout the night. The prisoners were interrogated once more and confronted with one another. All were condemned.

The last picture that we have of Bonhoeffer comes from the prison doctor, who wrote many years later:

"On the morning of the day, some time between five and six o'clock, the prisoners, among them Admiral Canaris, General Oster and Sack the Judge Advocate General, were led out of their cells and the verdicts read to them. Through the half-open door of a room in one of the huts I saw Pastor Bonhoeffer, still in his prison clothes, kneeling in fervent prayer to the Lord his God. The devotion and evident conviction of being heard that I saw in the prayer of this intensely captivating man moved me to the depths."

So the morning came. Now the prisoners were ordered to strip. They were led down a little flight of steps under the trees to the secluded place of execution. There was a pause. For the men about to die, time hung a moment suspended. Naked under the scaffold in the sweet spring woods, Bonhoeffer knelt for the last time to pray. Five minutes later, his life was ended.

—Mary Bosanquet, *The Life and Death of Dietrich Bonhoeffer,*
pp. 270–272, 276–278

The following letter was written by a twenty-five-year-old Danish seaman two days before his death at the hands of the Gestapo.

VESTRE PRISON
GERMAN SECTION
CELL 411
4 April 1945

MY OWN LITTLE DARLING.

Today I was taken before the military tribunal and condemned to death. What a terrible blow this is for a little girl of twenty! I've been given permission to write this farewell letter, but what shall I write? How shall I formulate my swan song? Time is short and there is so much to say.

What is the final and most precious thing I can give you? What do I possess that I can leave you as a parting gift so that in spite of your loss you will smile and go on living and developing?

We sailed on a stormy sea, we met in the trusting way of playing children and we loved each other. We still love each other and always will, but one day a storm separated us. I went aground while you were washed up on shore, and you are going to continue living in a new world. I don't expect you to forget me. Why should you forget something so beautiful as that which existed between us? But you mustn't become a slave to this memory. You must keep on going with the same easy and graceful approach to life as before and twice as happy because on your way Life gave you one of its greatest gifts. Free yourself—let this greatest of joys be everything to you, let it shine brighter and clearer than anything else, but let it be only one of your most treasured memories. Don't let it blind you and keep you from seeing all the wonderful things life has in store for you. Don't be unhappy, my dearest one. You must mature and grow rich in inner resources. Do you understand this, my beloved?

You will live on and you will have other beautiful adventures, but promise me—this you owe to everything I have lived for—that never will the thought of me come between you and Life. Remember, I will continue to live in your heart, but the part of me which remains there should be sound and natural and mustn't take up too much room. Gradually as bigger and more important things appear, I shall glide into the background and be a tiny speck of the soil out of which your happiness and your development will keep on growing.

Now you are heartbroken and this is what is known as sorrow, but Hanne, look beyond this. All of us are going to die and it isn't for us to judge whether my going a little earlier is good or bad.

I keep on thinking about Socrates. Read him and you will find Plato expressing what I feel at this moment. My love for you is without bounds, but not more so now than before. It's not a love which causes me pain. This is the way it is, and I want you to understand it. There is something inside me alive and growing—an inspiration, a love—call it what you like; something which I still haven't been able to define. Now I'm going to die and I still don't know if I have started a little flame in another being, a flame which will survive me. But still, my mind is at rest because I've seen the richness and abundance of nature. No one takes notice if a few seeds are trampled under and die. When I see all the riches that still live on, why should I despair?

Lift up your head, my most precious love, and look! The sea is still blue, the sea which I loved and which has enveloped us both. Now you will live for the two of us. I am gone and what remains is not a memory which will make you into a woman like S., but mold you into a woman living and warm, mature and happy. This does not mean that you are to try to rise above sorrow, because then you will become rigid and assume a saintly attitude with regard to your faith in me and in your self, and you will lose what I most loved in you—that you are first and last and always a woman.

Remember—and I swear this is true—that all sorrow gradually turns into happiness. But few are those who admit it when the time comes. They cloak themselves in mourning; habit makes them think that it is sorrow, and so they continue to cloak themselves in it. The truth is that after suffering comes maturity and after this maturity the fruits are gathered.

You see, Hanne, one day you will meet the man who will be your husband. The thought of me will flash through you, and you will perhaps deep down have a vague, uneasy feeling that you are betraying me or something in you which is pure and sacred. Lift up your head once more, Hanne, look straight into my eyes which are smiling at you and you will understand that the only way to betray me is by not completely following your natural instincts. When you see him, let your heart go out to meet him—not to drown your sorrow but because you truly love him. You will be very, very happy because you now have a base on which feelings still unknown to you will nurture.

Greet Nitte for me. I've thought of writing her but don't know if I'll have the time. I seem to feel as if I could do more for you because all that is life to me is now concentrated on you. I would like to breathe into you all the life that is in me, so that it can go on and as little as possible of it go to waste. This is the way I was made.
—Kim Malthe-Bruun, *Heroic Heart,* pp. 164–167

An extract from Father Delp's prison diary written in the days just before his death sentence was passed:

BUT ONE THING is gradually becoming clear—I must surrender myself completely. This is seed time, not harvest. God sows the seed and some time or other he will do the reaping. The one thing I must do is to make sure the seed falls on fertile ground. And I must arm myself against the pain and depression that sometimes almost defeat me. If this is the way God has chosen—and everything indicates that it is—then I must willingly and without rancor make it my way. May others at some future time find it possible to have a better and happier life because we died in this hour of trial.

I ask my friends not to mourn, but to pray for me and help me as long as I have need of help. And to be quite clear in their own minds that I was sacrificed, not conquered. It never occurred to me that my life would end like this. I had spread my sails to the wind and set my course for a great voyage, flags flying, ready to brave every storm that blew. But it could be they were false flags or my course wrongly set or the ship a pirate and its cargo contraband. I don't know. And I will not sink to cheap jibes at the world in order to raise my spirits. To be quite honest I don't want to die, particularly now that I feel I could do more important work and deliver a new message about values I have only just discovered and understood. But it has turned out otherwise. God keep me in his providence and give me strength to meet what is before me.

It only remains for me to thank a great many people for their help and loyalty and belief in me, and for the love they have shown me. First and foremost my brethren in the Order who gave me a genuine and beautiful vision of life. And the many sincere people I was privileged to meet. I remember very clearly the times when we were able to meet freely and discuss the tasks in front of us. Do not give up, ever. Never cease to cherish the people in your hearts —the poor forsaken and betrayed people who are so helpless. For in spite of all their outward display and loud self-assurance, deep down they are lonely and frightened. If through one man's life there is a little more love and kindness, a little more light and truth in the world, then he will not have lived in vain.

Nor must I forget those to whom I owe so much. May those I have hurt forgive me—I am sorry for having injured them. May those to whom I have been untrue forgive me—I am sorry for having failed them. May those to whom I have been proud and overbearing forgive me—I repent my arrogance. And may those to whom I have been unloving forgive me—I repent my hardness. Oh yes—long hours spent in this cell with fettered wrists and my body and spirit tormented must have broken down a great deal that was hard in me. Much that was unworthy and worthless has been committed to the flames.

So farewell. My offense is that I believed in Germany and her eventual emergence from this dark hour of error and distress, that I refused to accept that accumulation of arrogance, pride and force that is the Nazi way of life, and that I did this as a Christian and a Jesuit. These are the values for which I am here now on the brink waiting for the thrust that will send me over. Germany will be reborn, once this time has passed, in a new form based on reality with Christ and his Church recognized again as being the answer to the secret yearning of this earth and its people, with the Order the home of proved men—men who today are hated because they are misunderstood in their voluntary dedication or feared as a reproach in the prevailing state of pathetic, immeasurable human bondage. These are the thoughts with which I go to my death.

And so to conclude I will do what I so often did with my fettered hands and what I will gladly do again and again as long as I have a breath left—I will give my blessing. I will bless this land and the people; I will bless the Church and pray that her fountains may flow again fresher and more freely; I will bless all those who have believed in me and trusted me, all those I have wronged and all those who have been good to me—often too good.

God be with you and protect you. Help my poor old parents through these days of trial and keep them in your thoughts. God help you all.

I will honestly and patiently await God's will. I will trust him till they come to fetch me. I will do my best to ensure that this blessing, too, shall not find me broken and in despair.

Alfred Delp, S.J., *The Prison Meditations of Father Delp,*
pp. 163–165

Glad Amen . . .
When the chorus
of I am's
surrender to
the solo—
He is.

　　　　—Alma Loftness

BIBLIOGRAPHY

Alexander, Sheila, *Eunice, The Minnesota Review.*
Berdyaev, Nicolas, *The Destiny of Man,* Harper & Row, 1960.
Berne, Eric, *Games People Play,* Grove Press, Inc., 1964.
Berrigan, Daniel, *No Bars to Manhood,* Doubleday & Company, Inc., 1970.
Bertine, Eleanor, *Jung's Contribution to Our Time,* G. P. Putnam's Sons, 1968.
Bettelheim, Bruno, *The Informed Heart,* The Macmillan Company, 1960.
Bonhoeffer, Dietrich, *Letters and Papers from Prison,* The Macmillan Company, 1953.
———, *Life Together,* Harper & Row, 1954.
Boorstin, Daniel J., *The Image, or What Happened to the American Dream,* Atheneum Publishers, 1961. (Also in Harper Colophon edition.)
Bosanquet, Mary, *The Life and Death of Dietrich Bonhoeffer,* Harper & Row, 1968.
Buber, Martin, *Tales of the Hasidim, Early Masters,* Schocken Books Inc., 1947.
———, *Tales of the Hasidim, Later Masters,* Schocken Books Inc., 1948.
———, *Ten Rungs: Hasidic Sayings,* Schocken Books Inc., 1947.
Bugental, J. F. T., *The Search for Authenticity,* Holt, Rinehart and Winston, Inc., 1965.
Churchill, Winston, Speech in the House of Commons, quoted in *The Oxford Dictionary of Quotations,* Oxford University Press, 1941.
Cosby, N. Gordon, a sermon.
Delp, Alfred, *The Prison Meditations of Father Alfred Delp,* Herder & Herder, 1963. (Also in Macmillan paperback edition.)

De Ropp, Robert S., *The Master Game.* A Seymour Lawrence Book/Delacorte Press, 1968. (Also in Dell paperback edition.)

De Unamuno, Miguel, *Tragic Sense of Life,* Dover Publications, Inc., 1921.

Dougall, Lily, *God's Way and Man,* Student Christian Movement Press, 1924.

Eliot, George, *Mr. Gilfil's Love-Story,* quoted in *The Oxford Dictionary of Quotations,* Oxford University Press, 1941.

Evely, Louis, *Suffering,* Herder & Herder, 1967.

Frankl, Viktor E., *The Doctor and the Soul,* Alfred A. Knopf, Inc., 1955. (Also in Bantam paperback edition.)

Freud, Sigmund, *On Creativity and the Unconscious,* Basic Books, 1959. (Also in Harper Torchbooks edition.)

Friedman, Maurice S., *Martin Buber, The Life of Dialogue,* University of Chicago Press, 1955. (Also in Harper Torchbooks edition.)

Gilkey, Langdon, *Shantung Compound,* Harper & Row, 1966.

Griffin, John Howard, "Creative Suffering," United Church Press, 1970.

Haines, John, *Winter News,* Wesleyan University Press, 1965.

Hammarskjöld, Dag, *Markings,* Alfred A. Knopf, Inc., 1964.

Hanna, Charles B., *The Face of the Deep,* The Westminster Press, 1948.

Harding, M. Esther, *The 'I' and the 'Not-I,'* Princeton University Press, 1965.

Hare, Julius Charles & Augustus William, *Guesses at Truth,* quoted in *The Oxford Dictionary of Quotations,* Oxford University Press, 1941.

Hayakawa, S. I., *Symbol, Status and Personality,* Harcourt Brace Jovanovich, Inc., 1963.

Horney, Karen, *New Ways in Psychoanalysis,* W. W. Norton & Company, Inc., 1939.

Howe, E. Graham and L. Le Mesurier, *The Open Way,* Vincent Stuart & John M. Watkins, Ltd., 1939.

Jung, C. J., *Collected Works,* Princeton University Press, 1959–1968.

Keen, Sam, *Apology for Wonder,* Harper & Row, 1969.

———, *To a Dancing God,* Harper & Row, 1970.

Kelly, Thomas R., *A Testament of Devotion,* Harper & Row, 1941.

Kierkegaard, Søren, *Journals,* Harper & Row, 1959.

———, *Purity of Heart Is to Will One Thing,* Harper & Row, 1938.

Kotschnig, Elined, "Creative Light," *Inward Light,* No. 39.

Landstrom, Elsie, "Song to My Other Self," *Inward Light,* No. 67.

Lester, Julius, *Search for the New Land,* The Dial Press, 1969.

Loomis, Earl A., Jr., *The Self in Pilgrimage,* Harper & Row, 1960.

Malthe-Bruun, Kim, *Heroic Heart,* Random House, 1955. (Also in Seabury Press paperback edition.)

Maugham, W. Somerset, *Of Human Bondage,* quoted in *The Oxford Dictionary of Quotations,* Oxford University Press, 1941.

Meister Eckhart, *Treatises and Sermons,* Harper & Row, 1958.

Menninger, Karl, *The Human Mind,* Alfred A. Knopf, 1930.

Miller, Arthur, *After the Fall,* The Viking Press, Inc., 1964.

Moustakas, Clark, *Creativity and Conformity,* Van Nostrand Reinhold Company, 1967.

Neumann, Erich, *Depth Psychology and a New Ethic,* G. P. Putnam's Sons, 1969.

Nicoll, Maurice, *Psychological Commentaries,* Vincent Stuart & John M. Watkins Ltd., 1964.

Oates, Wayne E., *Anxiety in Christian Experience,* The Westminster Press, 1955.
———, *The Holy Spirit in Five Worlds,* Association Press, 1968.
———, *Religious Dimensions of Personality,* 1957.
Ouspensky, P. D., *In Search of the Miraculous,* Harcourt, Brace & World, Inc., 1969.
Paton, Alan, "The Challenge of Fear," *Saturday Review,* Sept. 9, 1967.
Potok, Chaim, *The Chosen,* Simon & Schuster, Inc., 1967. (Also in Fawcett Crest Book Edition.)
Reece, Roland R., *Notes from a Journal,* Shadybrook House. Vol. 12, No. 1, 1969.
Reik, Theodor, *The Search Within,* Farrar, Straus & Giroux, Inc., 1956. (Also in Funk and Wagnalls paperback edition.)
Rogers, Carl, "Person to Person: The Problem of Being Human," Real People Press, 1967. (Also in Delta Dell paperback edition.)
Rogers, Raymond, *Coming into Existence: The Struggle to Become an Individual,* The World Publishing Company, 1967.
Rusk, Howard A., "Light in Darkness," *The New York Times,* Jan. 4, 1969.
Sampson, R. V. *The Psychology of Power,* Pantheon Books, 1965. (Also in Vintage paperback edition.)
Sanders, J. A., Joseph, Our Brother, a sermon.
Schutz, Roger, *The Power of the Provisional,* Pilgrim Press, 1969.
Shiflett, Bill, "Community, Commitment and Judgment in Mission," a paper.
Storr, Anthony, *The Integrity of Personality,* Atheneum Publishers, 1961. (Also in Penguin Books edition.)
St. Teresa, *Collected Works,* Sheed & Ward, Inc., 1946.
Stanley, David M., *A Modern Scriptural Approach to the Spiritual Exercises,* Loyola University Press, 1967.
Tietjens, Eunice, "A Plaint of Complexity," *The Dial,* May 31, 1919.
Trueblood, Elton, *The New Man for Our Time,* Harper & Row, 1970.
Weinberg, George, *The Action Approach,* The World Publishing Company, 1967.
Wickes, Frances G., *The Inner World of Choice,* Harper & Row, 1963.
Williams, Daniel Day, *The Spirit and the Forms of Love,* Harper & Row, 1968.
Williams, H. A., *The True Wilderness,* J. B. Lippincott Company, 1965.
Wyon, Olive, *The Altar Fire,* SCM Press Ltd., 1954. (Also in Allenson paperback edition.)